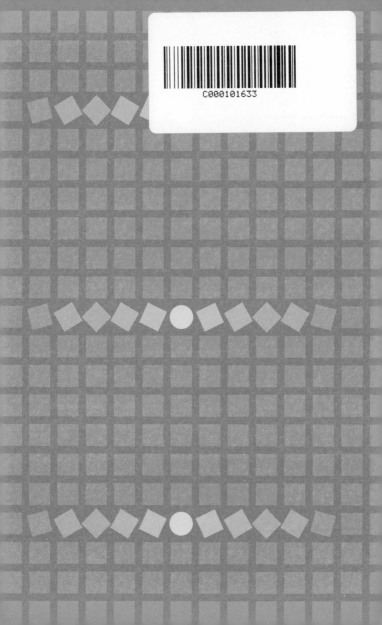

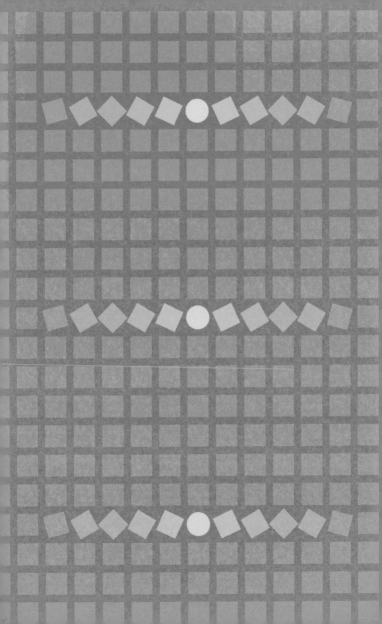

ADVANCE PRAISE

———

"What does success look like? Ask a million people and they will give you a million different answers. Many answers will centre around making as much money as possible. But meaningful success requires an understanding of some key human values. Neil Francis understands this well and his latest book gives important insights into how to combine business or personal success and human impact at the same time. Neil has an insightful and important story to tell which will certainly encourage inspired thinking."

Mel Young, President, Homeless World Cup

"Neil is an inspiration himself. His books knit together theory and practice in a way that is both easy to follow and to adopt. And why would we not wish to adopt practices that add value, encourage creativity and inspire others? Unlike some books which use global phenomena as case studies, Neil's latest book uses realistic, close-to-home examples which enable the reader to empathize with the protagonists and identify with the situation, thus encouraging changes in behaviour which in turn help to deliver success."

Malcolm Cannon, National Director, IoD Scotland

"What is 'inspiration?' How can inspiration propel you to achieve remarkable things, even in the face of extreme adversity? How can you see new possibilities when the odds are stacked against you? How can you use 'bad luck' to enrich your life and find deeper meaning and purpose? How does inspiration relate to motivation and passion?

"In this wonderful book, Neil Francis explores these questions through examples of inspirational people. With optimism, positivity, gentleness and understanding, he provides useful, practical tips, tools and strategies to find inspiration and propel us to a life full of deeper meaning, purpose and satisfaction."

Gillian Mead, Professor of Stroke and Elderly Care Medicine, University of Edinburgh

"I did not know the real meaning of the word 'inspiring' until I came into contact with stroke survivors when I myself suffered a major stroke at only 48 years old. Neil is an inspiration in his own right, and his new book shares the stories of numerous people who inspire us with their real life experiences; all told through the eyes of someone who knows what he is talking about."

Michael Lynagh, Managing Director, Dow Jones Corporate, and former Australian rugby player and World Cup Winner 1991

"Knowing how find sources of inspiration from the world around you is the key to ongoing motivation and happiness in life. *Inspired Thinking* has lots of practical tips on how to do just that."

Nicole Soames, CEO, Diadem Performance, and bestselling author, *The Coaching Book*

"Neil Francis has an eye for a motivating story. Thought-provoking, helpfully short and pithily expressed, the reader arrives rapidly at practical action that they can implement straight away.

"The result is indeed inspirational, so treat yourself to some inspired thinking."

Kevin Duncan, Bestselling author, *The Intelligent Work Book*

"I have known a number of inspirational people in my life and Neil is right up there with the best of them. Overcoming adversity is one thing, but to do it in his way is a truly amazing experience to witness. He wants individuals to strive for – and to achieve – fulfilment in their lives and then pass that onto others. That is truly inspirational. He's a true 21ˢᵗ century role model."

Craig Paterson, Chairman, Globalcelt

Published by
LID Publishing Limited
The Record Hall, Studio 304,
16-16a Baldwins Gardens,
London EC1N 7RJ, UK

info@lidpublishing.com
www.lidpublishing.com

A member of:

businesspublishersroundtable.com

© Neil Francis, 2020
© LID Publishing Limited, 2020

Printed by CPI Group (UK) Ltd, Croydon CR0 4YY
ISBN: 978-1-912555-77-2

Cover and page design: Caroline Li

INSPIRED
THINKING

HOW TO DISCOVER NEW IDEAS
FOR MEANINGFUL SUCCESS

NEIL FRANCIS

MADRID | MEXICO CITY | LONDON
NEW YORK | BUENOS AIRES
BOGOTA | SHANGHAI | NEW DELHI

In memory of my friend Howie,
one of life's good guys

"ONE DAY YOU WILL WAKE UP AND THERE WON'T BE ANY MORE TIME TO DO THE THINGS YOU'VE ALWAYS WANTED. DO IT NOW."

Paulo Coelho

TO START, A STORY
TO GET YOU IN
THE RIGHT MOOD
FOR MY BOOK

———

A philosophy professor stands in front of his class. Wordlessly, he picks up a large, empty glass jar and proceeds to fill it with golf balls. He then asks his students whether the jar is full. They agree that it is.

The professor then picks up a box of pebbles and pours these into the jar too. He shakes the jar lightly, and the pebbles fall into the spaces between the golf balls. He again asks the students again if the jar is full, and they agree that it is.

Next, the professor picks up a box containing sand and pours this into the jar. Of course, the sand fills up the remaining gaps. He asks once more if the jar is full and the students respond with a unanimous 'yes.'

The professor then produces two bottles of beer from under the table and pours their entire contents into the jar, effectively filling the tiny spaces between the grains of sand. The students laugh.

"Now," the professor says, as the laughter subsides, "I want you to recognize that this jar represents your life. The golf balls are the important things – your family, your health, your friends and your favourite passions – and if everything else was lost and only they remained, your life would still be full.

"The pebbles are the other things that matter, like perhaps your job and your house. The sand is everything else – the small stuff.

"If you put the sand into the jar first," he continues, "there's no room for the pebbles or the golf balls. The same goes for life. If you spend all your time and energy on the small stuff, you'll never have room for the things that are important to you. Pay attention to the things that are critical to your happiness.

"Spend time with your children. Spend time with your parents. Visit your grandparents. Take your spouse out to dinner. Play another 18 holes of golf. There will always be time to clean the house and mow the lawn.

"Take care of the golf balls first – the things that really matter. Set your priorities. The rest is just sand."

One of the students raises her hand and enquires what the beer represents. The professor smiles and says, "I'm glad you asked. The beer shows you that, no matter how full your life may seem, there's always room for a couple of beers with a friend."

CONTENTS

1	Acknowledgments	
2	Introduction	The rucksack
12	PART 1	LAYING THE FOUNDATION TO FIND INSPIRATION
15	Chapter 1	**What are the odds** Personal value
27	Chapter 2	**Think different** Individuality
37	Chapter 3	**The minority** Risk
48	PART 2	BLOCKING THE PATH TO DISCOVERING INSPIRATION
51	Chapter 4	**Invisible barriers** Blind self
63	Chapter 5	**Faking it** Self-belief
77	Chapter 6	**The focusing illusion** Triviality

86	PART 3	IDEAS THAT LEAD TO THE SOURCES OF INSPIRATION
89	Chapter 7	**Brilliant Hannah** Leading with purpose
99	Chapter 8	**Spirit of adventure** Staying young
109	Chapter 9	**Running Nick** Getting proactive
122	Chapter 10	**The rowing marine** Being determined
131	Chapter 11	**The heroic Rwandan** Identifying your heroes
144	Chapter 12	**Friends and parachutes** Seeking to collaborate
157	Chapter 13	**Formulas and tricks** Setting the right goals
168	Chapter 14	**Random events** Accepting luck
178	Chapter 15	**Leaving things behind** The right legacy

189	References and resources
195	About the author
196	About the book

ACKNOWLEDGMENTS

A massive thanks to:

Linda and Michael Henderson who allowed me to share their daughter Becca's story, which inspired me to write the book.

Fiona MacIver who read the first draft of the manuscript and helped give clarity around the core messages in the book.

The brilliant team at LID Publishing, especially Martin Lui, Susan Furber, Caroline Li, Francesca Stainer, Arabella Derhalli, Brian Doyle and Osaro Ewansiha.

My long suffering wife, Louise, who has to read every page of my manuscript and did the first proper edit, as has she has done with all my other previous books.

My children, Jack, Lucy and Sam for their support and love.

Finally, as always, my daft Golden Retrievers, Dougal and Archie, whose long walks on the beaches of North Berwick provided me the space and environment to plan the book.

To all of you, a big hug of gratitude.

INTRODUCTION

THE RUCKSACK

After that amusing anecdote, it might seem strange to launch into a book about inspirational thinking with a sad story, but bear with me through the next page or two. It will all make sense.

This is the story of an incredibly brave, positive and inspiring young lady named Becca Henderson. If you read my last book, *Positive Thinking*, I introduced her to you there. I knew of Becca because her dad, Michael, was a close school friend of mine and we stayed in touch over the years.

In 2017, at the age of 23, Becca was diagnosed with a rare form of heart cancer. The doctors tried to treat it with chemotherapy and radiation, but to no avail. The only path left to save Becca was for the doctors to remove her heart. And that is what they did.

But Becca didn't receive a biological heart from a transplant donor. Instead, she was given a Total Artificial Heart (TAH), a life-supporting cardiac system with an external mechanical driver and tubes that went into her abdomen. She carried it in a rucksack on her back.

Even with all of this going on in her life, Becca was always full of optimism, positivity and hope.

Before her operation, she regularly updated her Facebook page, sharing her thoughts and experiences of living with cancer of the heart. When she became very ill and was in intensive care, her parents kept the updates coming, allowing family and friends to stay abreast of how things were progressing. Then, she went through the operation to remove her heart and replace it with the TAH.

Over the months that followed, she made a fantastic recovery and again started to personally post Facebook updates on her progress.

Through all of this, she had been determined not to allow her condition to rule her life.

Every time I saw a Facebook update with Becca sitting in a restaurant, or out with her friends, or playing with her dog in the garden, it blew my mind that she actually had no biological heart, and yet was 'living' as normal a life as possible!

In 2018, she resumed her Master's course at the University of Oxford and went to classes carrying her TAH in its rucksack. She even applied to do a PHD at Oxford and her proposal was accepted.

I marvelled time and again at Becca's bravery, resilience and positive attitude in the face of everything she had to deal with.

And then, in early 2019, she was told by the doctors that a suitable heart had been found. The operation initially seemed to be a success, but things quickly took a turn for the worse. Six days later – on 27 February – Becca died.

Even though it was incredibly sad, in the weeks and months after her death, I became more and more inspired by her life. The same could be said of vast numbers of family, friends and people she'd never even met, as was evident from comments posted on her Facebook page. Her story made the front page of the BBC website and many local and national newspapers wrote articles about her.

Oxford awarded her Master's degree posthumously, a decision the university made based on her progress toward successfully completing a degree in English. Her tutors noted,

"Becca was a person of extraordinary courage, humour and intellectual achievement."

Everybody who knew her, or had heard of what she'd gone through, was inspired by her story.

Above all, it was Becca's resilience that stood out. Whatever life threw at her, she would bounce back with her positive attitude. That resilience, in turn, inspired me to think of ways I could be more resilient in my own life. And that sparked the idea for this book, as a way to share sources of inspiration that others can draw from.

When someone or something inspires you, it can push you to do something new or different. It gives you new ideas, and strong feelings of enthusiasm and excitement, and you feel energized. This is the key point of this book. I'm confident you'll be inspired by the ideas in these pages, which you can harness and translate into meaningful success. This will help you discover new strategies and ideas for achieving the goals and objectives you set, pushing your own boundaries and addressing difficult challenges, setbacks and obstacles in a far more positive way.

However, it is important to understand that *the application* of these ideas and strategies will always be more powerful than the ideas themselves. The key to getting the most out of this book is to apply an idea or a strategy that inspires you in your life, and actively use it. The best inspiration comes from the application of ideas, not the consumption of them.

"The inspiration is not the receiving of information," wrote the entrepreneur, musician and TED Talk speaker Derek Sivers. "The inspiration is applying what you've received."

Each chapter of this book starts with a story from the life of an individual that encapsulates the importance of a particular theme. This is backed up by various sources of inspiration, including practical examples, tips, tools and strategies that will help you harness all of this to achieve meaningful success.

Along the way, we'll explore ideas around personal value, individuality, risk, 'the blind self,' self-belief, triviality, purpose, staying young, proactivity, determination, heroes, goals, collaboration, being lucky and legacy. They are ideas that will inform your way of thinking and inspire you to achieve success.

First, a brief word about 'success.' When I talk about success, I don't mean material success, even though that could be a by-product. Instead, I'm referring to accomplishment of those things that give you purpose, meaning and fulfilment. That might focus mainly on what you do – your occupation – or it could be volunteering, family, friendship or another form of success.

As for my part, I am an entrepreneur and an author, not a psychologist or a social scientist. I don't have a PhD and don't employ researchers. What I try to do is interpret and condense what I think are interesting, relevant and useful bits of information that others can benefit from. This information is drawn from what I read, podcasts, webinars, seminars and dialogue with relevant experts.

As I have explored the world of 'Inspired Thinking,' I've tried to ensure that the examples, case studies, methods and tools referenced in this book are based on scientific evidence. Having said that, I'm grateful to all the researchers, scientists, psychologists, entrepreneurs and explorers I've drawn my material from.

> "THE MOST IMPORTANT THING IS TO TRY AND INSPIRE PEOPLE SO THAT THEY CAN BE GREAT IN WHATEVER THEY WANT TO DO."

Kobe Bryant

IMPORTANCE
OF INSPIRATION

———

Before we start, and for clarity, it is important to explain the difference between inspiration and motivation. Although they have two very distinct meanings, these terms are often used interchangeably.

Inspiration is something that you feel on the inside, while motivation is something exerted from the outside that compels you to take action. Inspiration is a 'driving force,' while motivation is a 'pulling force.'

Inspiration lasts longer than motivation. Motivation will get you through the workday, or help you achieve a specific goal, but it won't last a lifetime. Inspiration is enduring. It can extend for a very long period of time, influencing all aspects of your life.

Inspiration comes from passion; motivation does not. Typically, when you're motivated to do something, you simply want to achieve that goal and move on. Inspiration is deeper than motivation. It stems from passion; from being influenced by something or someone in such a way that you want to change things and do things. Motivation, in the moment, can seem powerful, but its power fades when compared to the brilliance that is inspiration.

Inspiration and passion are closely linked to one another. You can be motivated without being passionate, but you rarely see inspiration without passion close by.

But what exactly is inspiration? When we think about it or talk about it, what do we actually mean when we say, "I feel inspired" or "That really inspired me?"

When you have the feeling of inspiration, there's a surge of energy, with a thrilling rush of elation and excitement. The senses are amplified, and you're far more aware of the possibilities that seem to be opening up for you. You enter a state of 'flow,' where you lose track of time. You don't feel self-conscious, but rather assured that what you're doing is intrinsically rewarding, purposeful and enjoyable.

In that special moment, it feels as though you have acquired some new perception, a new way to see things. This leads to a burst of energy, and true inspiration gives us motivation and liveliness to take action.

The word itself comes from the Latin *inspirare*, meaning 'to breath into.' One inspirational achievement – say, to land a probe on Mars – has a tendency to raise the sense of possibility in others. It could, for instance, compel a teenage boy to study astronomy at university or excite an adolescent girl who dreams of becoming an astronaut. The one who is inspired eventually performs their own feats, and inspires others, and so on down the line.

Finding inspiration from a person, a team, a piece of art, a scientific solution or the wonders of nature brings with it a wave of energy that by itself can propel you to start doing things you may not have thought possible. It's so important because it keeps the mind positive and focused on the bigger picture.

Dr Scott Kaufman, a Columbia University psychologist, explored the phenomenon in "Why Inspiration Matters," an article in *The Harvard Business Review*.

"In a culture obsessed with measuring talent and ability, we often overlook the important role of inspiration," he wrote. "Inspiration awakens us to new possibilities by allowing us to transcend our ordinary experiences and limitations. Inspiration propels a person from apathy to possibility and transforms the way we perceive our own capabilities."

Psychologists Todd Thrash and Andrew Elliot, of the University of Rochester in Upstate New York, have been studying inspiration for decades. They've identified three things that occur when we're inspired: we see new possibilities; we're receptive to an outside influence; and we feel energized and motivated.

Fortunately, inspiration is not a static state of mind, but a process you can cultivate. While we can't force ourselves to be inspired, we can create an environment that's conducive to inspiration.

And this is the 'environment' I want to create in this book, which grew out of the inspiration I found in how Becca lived her life. Hopefully the stories, the ideas, the insights and the suggestions will inspire you to achieve meaningful and rewarding success.

Not a bad legacy. In fact, I think it is a brilliant and inspiring one.

PART 1

LAYING THE FOUNDATION TO FIND INSPIRATION

"IT IS NEVER
TOO LATE TO BE
WHO YOU MIGHT
HAVE BEEN."

George Eliot

CHAPTER 1
WHAT ARE THE ODDS

PERSONAL VALUE

In May 2015, three teachers at Buckton Vale Primary School, in Greater Manchester, England – Deborah Brown, Kelly Quinn and Jenny Brierley – sent a letter to all Year 6 pupils. The communiqué went out a week before the children were to sit their Standard Assessment Tests (SATs), which in the UK are used to evaluate educational progress.

From personal experience, I can tell you that most parents dread getting a letter from their children's school. It usually means that their child has done something wrong, or has a bad attendance record. But this was a letter of a very different type.

It told the youngsters how special and unique they were. It highlighted all the natural skills and abilities they possessed, and everything that made them smart individuals.

They were told how their laughter could brighten the darkest day, and that the SAT examiners didn't know how kind, trustworthy and thoughtful they truly were.

This is the text of that letter, which was reprinted by newspapers and websites, and shared globally across social media:

Dear Year 6 pupils,

Next week you will sit your SATs tests for maths, reading, spelling, grammar and punctuation. We know how hard you have worked, but there is something very important you must know:

The SATs test does not assess all of what makes each of you special and unique. The people who create these tests and score them do not know each of you the way that we do and certainly not in the way your families do.

They do not know that some of you speak two languages or that you love to sing or draw.

They have not seen your natural talent for dancing or playing a musical instrument.

They do not know that your friends can count on you to be there for them; that your laughter can brighten the darkest day or that your face turns red when you feel shy.

They do not know that you participate in sports, wonder about the future, or sometimes help your little brother or sister after school. They do not know that you are kind, trustworthy and thoughtful and that every day you try to be your very best.

The levels you will get from this test will tell you something, but they will not tell you everything. There are many ways of being smart. You are smart! So while you are preparing for the test and in the midst of it all, remember that there is no way to 'test' all of the amazing and awesome things that make you, YOU!

It ends with a quotation from Aristotle: "Educating the mind without educating the heart is no education at all."

What a brilliant letter!

Yes, exams are important. But as the letter highlights so well, there is so much more to a child's makeup than being successful (or not) in exams. It's all about a child being valued, and that's why what these teachers did was – and continues to be – so inspiring.

The message of encouragement tapped into a basic human need: being valued for who you are. It's not about your income, your qualifications, your job, the type of car youdrive, where you live or whom you know, but about being valued for *just being you*. This letter spotlighted the notion that every child is to be respected and appreciated for who they are, regardless of ability.

"THE DEEPEST PRINCIPLE IN HUMAN NATURE IS THE CRAVING TO BE APPRECIATED."

William James

THE UNIQUENESS
OF YOU

———

One of the most inspiring ideas you can ever have is when you realize that you're a unique human being. There is nobody else on earth like you. You are one of a kind, and you should therefore start to value and appreciate yourself more. You were born and you are alive and you're wonderful just the way you are.

Perhaps the following examples will help you to appreciate the uniqueness of *you*.

As author Mel Robbins explains, there was about a one in 400 trillion chance of you being born as 'you.' This is the probability of you being born when and where you were, to your particular parents, with your distinct genetic makeup.

Dr Ali Benazir, an author who studied at Harvard, received a medical degree from the University of California, San Diego, and studied philosophy at Cambridge University, expanded upon Robbins' thought.

He worked out the odds of your parents meeting, given the billions of men and women populating our planet. He then pondered how many people of the opposite sex your mother and father would have met in their first 25 years of life. Next, he looked at the chances of them talking, meeting again, forming a long-term relationship, having kids together, and the right egg and the right sperm combining to make 'you.' He went even further back to look at the probability of all your ancestors mating, and of all the right sperm meeting all the right eggs, to produce each one of those ancestors.

Benazir's conclusion: "The odds that you exist at all are basically zero."

He explained it this way: "It is the probability of two million people getting together, each to play a game of dice with trillion-sided dice. They each roll the dice and they all come up with the exact same number – for example, 550,343,279,001. A miracle is an event so unlikely as to be almost impossible. By that definition, I've just shown that you are a miracle. Now go forth and feel and act like the miracle that you are."

So, please be inspired that 'you' were even born at all!

YOU BELONG TO A UNIQUE AND FANTASTIC SPECIES

If an alien in a UFO arrived in our atmosphere and observed our planet, there's no doubt that among the millions of species on Earth, homo sapiens would stand out. We are at the top of the food chain, we've tamed and extended our habitats over the entire planet, and in recent centuries we created an explosion of technological, engineering, societal and artistic advancements.

It's remarkable how far we've come in what, from an evolutionary perspective, has been a very short period of time.

Evolutionary biologist Richard Dawkins has a superb analogy to highlight this fact: Stretch your arms out to represent the span of the history of life on Earth, from the origins of life to where we are today. With this scale, the whole history of our species is represented by the thickness of one fingernail clipping. All of *recorded* human history is represented by the dust from one light stroke of a nail file.

Of all the species that have ever lived on Earth, 99.9% are now extinct. One can't help but wonder: how did our species ever get so far? Not only have we survived, but we've achieved intellectual and technological progress beyond any other form of life on the planet.

So, what is it that makes us unique?

First, it's our ability to think abstractly about objects, principles and ideas that are not physically present. We can imagine doing things in the future, like planning a holiday or attending a sporting or cultural event. We can communicate through writing, talking and drawing.

Our genes rely on procreation to be passed on, but memes – units of cultural information spread by imitation – can be transmitted much faster, through writing, speech, gestures or rituals. Memes facilitate cumulative knowledge and experiences that can serve as a powerful force for human progress.

Many of mankind's inventions have helped us transcend our biology. Philosophers Andy Clark of the University of Edinburgh and David Chalmers of New York University, who put forth 'The Theory of the Extended Mind,' describe how we use technology to push the boundaries of human consciousness beyond our skulls. We use tools like computers and smartphones to enhance our cognitive skills, or powerful telescopes to extend our visual reach. Technology has become a part of our exoskeleton, they argue, allowing us to push beyond our limitations.

The very fact that we as human beings can write, read and contemplate the unique nature of our mental abilities is awe-inspiring. It is inspiring to even think that you are an individual who belongs to such a fantastic species.

VS Ramachandran, a professor of neuroscience at the University of California, San Diego, perhaps said it best: "Here is this three-pound mass of jelly you can hold in the palm of your hand. It can contemplate the meaning of infinity, and it can contemplate itself contemplating the meaning of infinity."

Hopefully these examples will help you to feel absolutely valued for who you are. The fact that you are alive and breathing, and that you're a part of a very special species, should blow your mind! So, stop measuring your self-worth by how much money you earn, what car you drive, where you send your children to school or where you live, and really appreciate who you actually are.

This simple act – valuing yourself – is the starting point for discovering inspiration, harnessing it and translating it into success. When you start to value yourself more, you're more likely to have a positive outlook on life in general. And that, in turn, makes you more likely to seek out sources of new inspiration.

Along the way, there are two other important factors that will lead you to that breakthrough experience: individuality and risk.

WHAT ARE THE ODDS?

START

LET'S START SMALL.
What is the probability of your dad meeting your mom?

But over 25 years, he probably met around 10,000 women.

Though the world was smaller 20 years ago, your dad *could have* met almost **200 million** of its women (go dad!)

So the odds that your mom was in this small group and met your dad is:

1 in 20,000

BUT WE KNOW HOW TRICKY LOVE CAN BE.
What is the probability that they stay together long enough to have kids?

It is a 1 in 10 chance that they talk to each other.

X

Also a 1 in 10 chance that they go on a second date.

X

Another 1 in 10 chance that they keep dating for a while.

X

And a coin toss if they stay together long enough for offspring.

Thus, the odds that your parents' meeting results in kids is: **1 in 2,000**

So far, the combined odds of you being here are: **1 in 40,000,000**

That is about the size of the population of California.

NOW THINGS ARE GOING TO GET PRETTY INTERESTING.

Why? Because we are about to deal with eggs and sperm, which come in large numbers.

Mom has about 100,000 eggs in her lifetime.

Dad makes about 4 trillion sperm during the years you could have been born.

[Sally.]

What are the odds that the 1 egg...

[Harry.]

... met the 1 sperm, which together made you (and not your brother)?

1 in 400,000,000,000,000,000 (1 in 400 quadrillion)

That is approximately the volume in cubic meters of the Atlantic Ocean (3.236×10^{17} cubic meters).

BUT WE'RE JUST GETTING STARTED.

Because your existence here, now, and on planet earth presupposes another supremely unlikely and utterly undeniable chain of events. Namely, **that every one of your ancestors lived to reproductive age** – going all the way back not just to the first *Homo sapiens*, first *Homo erectus* and *Homo habilis*, but all the way back to the first single-celled organism. You are a representative of an unbroken lineage of life going back 4 billion years.

(You. Aw.)

1 in 2 odds that a child will be born, grow, and reproduce per generation...

What are the odds that your lineage remained unbroken for the length of human existence?

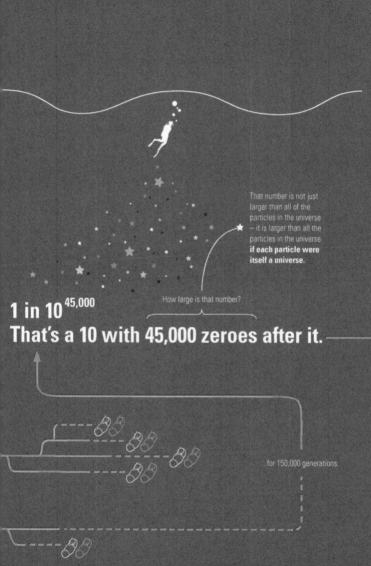

That number is not just larger than all of the particles in the universe – it is larger than all the particles in the universe **if each particle were itself a universe.**

How large is that number?

1 in 10 ^{45,000}
That's a 10 with 45,000 zeroes after it.

...for 150,000 generations.

(Weeeee!)

That is 1 quadrillion multiplied by 1 quadrillion for every generation.

THAT'S PRETTY BIG – BUT WAIT A MINUTE.
The right sperm also had to meet the right egg for every single one of those ancestors.

ODDS OF THE RIGHT SPERM, MEETING THE RIGHT EGG 150,000 TIMES?

$$1 \text{ in } 10^{2,640,000}$$

LET'S ADD IT ALL UP

$$10^{2,640,000} \times 10^{45,000} \times 2000 \times 20,000 \approx$$

$$1 \text{ in } 10^{2,685,000}$$

BY COMPARISON:

The number of atoms in the body of an average male (80kg, 175 lb) is about: 10^{27}

The number of atoms making up the earth is about: 10^{50}

The number of atoms in the known universe is estimated at: 10^{80}

THINK OF IT LIKE THIS:
It is the probability of 2 million people getting together (about the population of San Diego) each to play a game of dice with trillion-sided dice. They each roll the dice, and they all come up with the exact same number – for example, 550,343,279,001.

SO, THE ODDS THAT EXIST AT ALL ARE:

Basically zero.

CHAPTER 2
THINK DIFFERENT
INDIVIDUALITY

In April of 1976, Steve Jobs and Steve Wozniak co-founded Apple, the bellwether tech company that just turned 44. Apple is, of course, one of the most valuable and admired companies in the world, having developed a series of amazing products that include the Mac, iPod, iPad and iPhone.

But it hasn't always been smooth sailing for the company. After the phenomenal success of the trailblazing Apple I and Apple II personal computers in the 1970s and early 1980s, Apple had some serious failures. The Apple III, Lisa and the Macintosh all failed for various reasons, and Jobs was sacked in 1985. Apple found itself struggling again in the early 1990s, and in 1996 the company's board convinced Jobs to return as CEO.

While Jobs and team were busy developing the new products that would revive the brand's fortunes, he wanted an ad campaign that would remind Apple's loyal fan base of the qualities that had made it great in the first place. He retained the ad agency TBWA/Chiat/Day, which crafted what would become one of the most talked-about campaigns ever. It revolved around a deceptively simple, grammatically clumsy slogan: 'Think Different.'

Rob Siltanen, the agency's creative director and managing partner, wrote one of the most famous commercials in history for Apple's 'Think Different' TV marketing campaign. He named it 'The Crazy Ones.'

Narrated by actor Richard Dreyfuss, the ad started out with an instantly memorable salute to counterculture icons, with black-and-white images of more than a dozen 20th century visionaries. Images of people like Albert Einstein, Amelia Earhart, John Lennon and Dr Martin Luther King, Jr, appeared alongside copy praising the power of bold ideas. It extolled 'the round pegs in the square holes' who see things differently and push the human race forward.

The campaign wasn't solely responsible for the reversal of Apple's fortunes, but it played an important role in rallying customers, employees and shareholders at a difficult time for the company. It reasserted the brand's goals and aspirations, and more importantly, it told the world that with Jobs now back at the helm, Apple had its mojo back.

I think the ad copy Siltanen wrote was brilliant, powerful and inspiring, primarily because, at its core, it promotes the characteristic of individuality. It's about not following the crowd, but rather sticking to what you believe in and making a difference.

It's all about examining the views and opinions you've accumulated or formulated over the course of your life, but which, deep down, you don't actually believe. Stop conforming! Start spending your time doing things that you know you'll excel at!

Basically, it is time to become one of the crazy ones, and to 'think different.'

WHY INDIVIDUALITY
IS INSPIRING

There are many reasons why individuality can be inspiring. It encourages innovation and creativity. It allows you to disregard conventions and boundaries. Individuals who aren't limited by notions of what can or can't be accomplished are able to view situations in a different light and devise innovative solutions to problems.

Similarly, a strong sense of individuality means not being swayed by the fears or doubts of others. Many are plagued by uncertainty and self-doubt, but seeing traits of individuality in others encourages people to address and conquer their fears. Those with a true sense of individuality are able to weigh potential risks and benefits for themselves, without considering what may be commonly accepted or discouraged in society.

Individuality also encourages others to try more innovative approaches. Those who see the success of an individual with a unique idea are often inspired to pursue their own endeavours.

By being 'yourself,' you're likely to be less stressed and anxious, leading you to experience positive emotions such as joy, compassion, optimism, happiness, kindness and enthusiasm. Positive emotions are not simply 'happy feelings' that we chase to feel momentary pleasure. They play a significant role in everyday life.

The benefits of positive emotions are well documented by Barbara Lee Fredrickson, a psychology professor at the University of North Carolina, Chapel Hill, who's a leading researcher in this field. Among the outcomes she's noted are living longer, being more resilient, experiencing better mental and physical health, and being more engaged.

THE STANFORD
PRISON
EXPERIMENT

Conversely, removing individuality or limiting it can have serious consequences. An infamous example of this is the Stanford Prison Experiment.

In 1971, Stanford University in northern California enrolled 24 men in a psychological experiment intended to show the effects of the power dynamic between guards and prisoners. It was played out in the basement of a school building that had been turned into a metaphorical prison for purposes of the study. Half the men played the role of prison guards and the other half assumed the role of prisoners.

It started by giving twelve of the men prison uniforms, which were essentially long shirts with numbers on them. They supposed to be put into the lockup for two weeks, but the study only lasted six days due to the severe psychological trauma experienced by the prisoners. This was not due to physical violence, which wasn't allowed. But other than that prohibition, the guards had been given complete power and were allowed to discipline the prisoners as they saw fit.

Setting the stage for what was to follow, the psychologists who conducted the experiment had stripped the prisoners of their individuality. The guards treated them all the same, they had a number instead of their name, and their long shirts looked more like dresses, which had the effect of emasculating them.

After a series of provocations, punishments and physical altercations – as the guards exhibit increasingly cruel behaviour – the prisoners literally began to act 'crazy.' They screamed, cursed and seemingly lost control.

Researchers concluded that this was brought on by de-individuation, a state where one becomes so immersed in the norms of the group as to lose any sense of individual identity and personal responsibility. The guards may have been so sadistic because they didn't feel that what happened was down to them personally – it was a group norm. The prisoners lost their sense of personal identity because of the uniform they wore.

After the fact, most of the guards found it difficult to believe that they'd behaved in such brutalizing ways. Many said they hadn't known they were capable of such behaviour. The prisoners, too, could not believe that they'd responded in the submissive, cowering, dependent way that they had. Several claimed to be normally quite assertive.

Obviously, this is an extreme example of what can happen if you lose your individuality completely. I am not suggesting that 'following the crowd' would lead to serious psychological outcomes. But, it does illustrate how powerful individuality is.

So, if you feel, in parts of your life, that you are not being true to yourself, how do you start to rediscover your individuality?

HOW TO BE
YOURSELF

Most of us are too concerned with what others think of us. As such, we may disguise or manipulate features of our personality to better assure that others aren't judgmental or adversely reactive to us. If you're overly worried about what others think of you, then you are more likely to manipulate your personality and communication, either to seek approval or avoid disapproval.

For most of us, revealing our true selves can feel like a huge risk now that we live in a world where everyone is presenting themselves online as interesting and attractive. Being yourself can feel risky, as your 'public' or 'social media' face is invariably not who you really are. If you start showing your true self, these people may indeed treat you differently, and that's a perceived risk. But if you have to hide who you really are to be around these people, you can end up feeling lost, lonely, or even worthless, with no deep connections with them.

That can be very difficult to manage. So, here are five simple ideas to help you start rediscovering your individuality.

1. **Accept yourself.**
   Whatever you've been through, the starting point to being yourself is to accept whatever situation you find yourself in and just accept who you are. Remember this from Chapter 1: you are a unique human being. There is nobody else on earth like you, and this is your 'now' – the reality of your life as it currently is.

   When you accept your 'now', you will find that a huge weight has been lifted from your shoulders. I realize that this will be incredibly difficult for some people, but the only alternative is to keep the status quo and put on an act, both in person and through your online persona.

2. **Identify negative self-talk.**
   When facing any given situation, the first step is often self-talk. This is the endless stream of unspoken thoughts that run through your head. These automatic thoughts can be positive or negative. Some of your self-talk comes from logic and reason, while some may arise from misconceptions and misunderstandings. A lot of this can be 'promoted' through what you view on conventional media and social media, and how you relate to it. So, simply limiting your media time can help reduce negative self-talk.

3. Focus on your strengths.

In addition to negative self-talk, you can also easily slide into the habit of focusing on your weaknesses instead of celebrating your strengths. Playing to your strengths will enhance your well-being, improve your performance at work, help you become more engaged and make you more likely to achieve your goals. Leveraging your strengths can increase your resilience, confidence and happiness.

4. Express who you really are.

What else stops you from being yourself? Mostly, it's fear of what others might think if you showed your true self. So, people try to show the best sides of themselves – or, a carefully crafted fantasy image – whether in the flesh or via their social media profiles. They put on this act, revealing only slivers of who they actually are.

But it's important that you express who you really are. You need to be genuine with yourself – and genuinely be yourself – because if you stop doing that, even for some of the time, you might start to forget who you really are deep down. Then, it will be very difficult to be the 'individual' you really want to be, on any level.

5. Be vulnerable.

Another important step to being yourself is showing your vulnerability. It's scary to be openly vulnerable. But to fully be yourself, you have to be your full array of selves. You can't just pick and choose the parts that you like; you can't just show the manicured, photoshopped version of yourself. You have to be vulnerable from time to time.

To start with, choose specific people or opportune moments to show your vulnerability. Whether you share your personal stories with everyone, or just a few, it will help you to be all of yourself, at least some of the time.

If you untether yourself from insecurity and fear, and value yourself by focusing on your strengths, which will allow you to become more vulnerable, this can set the stage for a self-empowered life. Freeing yourself from worrying about what others think of you emboldens you to be sincerely genuine, which leads you to be far more open to new sources of inspiration.

So, become authentic, join the 'crazy' ones and reclaim your individuality.

CHAPTER 3
THE MINORITY

RISK

Let me introduce you to someone who you've likely never heard of, but his invention made the world a safer place.

Dr David Warren is an Australian scientist whose specialty is rocket science. In the 1950s he worked for a part of Australia's Defence Department that was focused on planes. In 1953, he was seconded to an expert panel trying to solve a costly and distressing mystery: why the British de Havilland Comet, the world's first commercial jet airliner and the great hope of the new 'Jet Age,' kept crashing.

The problem was that there were dozens of possible causes, and nothing but death and debris as evidence. "People were rattling on about staff training and pilots' errors, and did a fin break off the tail, and all sorts of things that I knew nothing about," Dr Warren recalled more than 50 years later.

"I found myself dreaming of something I'd seen the week before at Sydney's first post-war trade fair," he said. "And that was claimed to be the first pocket recorder, the Miniphon. There'd been nothing before like it."

The Miniphon was marketed as a dictation machine for businessmen, who could sit at their desks and record the contents of letters that would later be typed up by their secretaries. Initially, Warren was only interested in the Miniphon so that he could make recordings of his favourite jazz musicians.

However, when one of his fellow scientists suggested the latest doomed Comet might have been hijacked, something clicked for Warren. What if every plane in the sky had a mini recorder in the cockpit? If it were tough enough to survive a crash, accident investigators would never be confused again, because they'd have minute-by-minute audio right up to the moment of the crash. At the very least, they'd know what the pilots had said and heard.

The idea fascinated him. Warren knew his idea for a cockpit recorder was a good one; but without official support there was little he could do about it.

He took a risk and decided to pitch his invention to his boss, who was intrigued and urged him to keep working on it… but discreetly. Since it wasn't a government-approved venture or a war-winning weapon, it couldn't be seen to take up precious lab time or money.

In fact, his boss said to him: "If I find you talking to anyone, including me, about this matter, I will have to sack you."

It was a sobering thought for a young man with a wife and two children. However, he decided to try and build the first prototype, using steel wire to store four hours of pilot voices and instrument readings. He also designed it to automatically erase older records, so it was reusable.

Warren's under-the-radar experiment would become the world's first 'black box' flight recorder. His prototype was hugely successful and went into full production. In 1960, Australia became the first country to make cockpit voice recorders mandatory. Today, black boxes are fireproof, ocean-proof, encased in steel, and compulsory on every commercial flight in the world.

It's impossible to say how many people owe their lives to data captured in the death throes of a failing plane, as engineering flaws were exposed and safety innovations followed. Warren risked losing his job because he was inspired by the potential outcome: saving lives. That, he concluded, was more important than keeping his job... and that's incredibly inspiring!

> "BUT WE ALSO BELIEVE IN TAKING RISKS, BECAUSE THAT'S HOW YOU MOVE THINGS ALONG."

Melinda Gates

THE MAJORITY OR
THE MINORITY?

Everyone has ambitions during their lifetime – dreams of working for themselves; taking a sabbatical to travel to a new part of the world; going back to university; writing a book; choosing to leave a job that provides no real satisfaction. Yet, most people find excuses for not taking risks that could help them achieve their ambition.

We all know the litany of excuses: I need to pay the mortgage. I'm planning to take my children on holiday this year. I want to buy a new car. I'll need money to do these things, so I can't afford to take the risk just now. And what if I fail… or even worse, if people laugh at me for trying? I couldn't deal with the humiliation. No, perhaps I'll think about it again after the children are a bit older.

So, the ambition is put on the back-burner until it disappears from your memory. Then, a few months or years later, a new ambition starts to form in your mind and the same cautious, doubtful pattern repeats itself. And so it happens – you join the unfortunate majority of people who, for whatever reason, do not achieve their ambitions.

As Albert Einstein said: "A ship is always safe at the shore, but that is not what it is built for." Most people stay in their own 'safe harbour,' not willing to take the risks that would allow them to set sail for promising new horizons.

So, how do you avoid becoming *one of them*? First, you need to understand that risk-takers are in the minority of the population. Most people are inherently risk-averse, so if you take risks on a regular basis, you'll be out of the mainstream. However, this is good news: you'll face less competition, so you'll be able to carve your own path, and in doing so you'll have an easier time standing out in the crowd.

Accept this and then it's all about understanding the benefits of taking the right risks, as not all risks are the same. Therefore, you should take risks with the following caveats:

- **You need to examine all the options.**
  Risk-taking isn't about jumping on every opportunity; it's about choosing the right ones. Fully explore all your options before settling on any decision.

- **Your risks need to be calculated.**
  Leonard C Green, an entrepreneurship mentor, is known for insisting, "Entrepreneurs are not risk-takers; they're calculated risk-takers." Your goal isn't to blindly risk your career, family and fortune, but to maximize your chances of success. Knowing the odds, as specifically as possible, is the key to choosing the right risks to take.

- **Accept that taking risks involves uncertainty and change.**
  By nature, taking a risk means challenging uncertainty and instituting change. Try and accept this, focusing on the positive outcomes that could occur.

- **Trying to eliminate risk is a guarantee of failure.**
  Mark Zuckerberg, the founder of Facebook, said, "The only strategy that is guaranteed to fail is not taking risks." If you refuse to take any risks in your life, you'll pass up every opportunity in front of you in favour of a stable, certain future. That stability may be comforting, but it won't provide you with growth or advancement on any level.

- **Remember that 'We've always done it this way' can be a very dangerous statement.**
  Bill Aulet, a senior lecturer at the Massachusetts Institute of Technology's Sloan School of Management, insists that doing things the way they've always been done is, counter-intuitively, "The most risky thing you can probably do."

So, why are risk-takers in the minority?

TAKING RISKS
IS SCARY

———

Merely understanding the benefits of risk-taking isn't enough. Most of us are inherently risk-averse. In the face of a risk, or a bad situation, the human brain is wired to imagine worst-case scenarios, which unfortunately stifles our productivity and makes us feel anxious and stressed.

Historically, this has been a good thing for our species. Sharpening our perception of risk keeps us away from dangerous territory and maximizes our chances of survival. But in the modern world, where most risks we might take aren't life threatening, that overactive imagination can do more harm than good.

You might guess that risk-taking behaviour is predetermined, whether through genetics or a person's upbringing, and to some extent you'd be correct. For example, a study published on the *nature.com* website showed evidence that cortisol and testosterone levels may be linked to higher risk-taking behaviour – and your hormones aren't something you can control.

However, there are some strategies you can use to make yourself more comfortable with taking risks in your daily life. The neuroscientist and leadership coach Dr Tara Swart has shown that our current risk aversion (or risk tolerance) is linked to how we've benefited from risks in the past. If you take a risk and it pays off, you physiologically respond by favouring risks in the future. The opposite is true if a risk doesn't pay off.

Accordingly, you can make yourself more comfortable with risk simply by taking more risks – even if they're small ones – in your daily life. As long as you're making intelligent risk choices (making sure your chances of a payoff are greater than 50%), eventually all those decisions will reinforce the benefits of taking a calculated risk, and you won't be as risk averse in the future.

There is also evidence to suggest that you can shape your way of thinking just by pretending that you think in a different way.

In 2016, Professor Kevin Dunbar and Dr Denis Dumas from the University of Maryland published a paper called "The Creative Stereotype Effect." They found that people solved problems more creatively when acting in ways consistent with their perception of what creative people would do. In other words, the 'Fake it 'til you make it' approach is rooted in reality. It seems that thinking like a risk-taker, and behaving like one, can make you more comfortable with taking risks in your daily life.

Is it easy to shift your perceptions so dramatically that you become a risk-taker after a lifetime of risk aversion? Absolutely not… but it is possible. And if you want to succeed in achieving your ambitions, you need to start taking more risks. Start today by making one risky decision or taking one risky action, even if its benefits or consequences are minimal. It will mark the start of a new habit that might someday help you achieve your loftiest ambitions.

By laying the foundation, you will become far more open to new sources of inspiration. And then, in order to harness that inspiration and use it to succeed, you need to: accept the uniqueness and the personal value of you; celebrate your individuality and think differently from the crowd while striving to be authentic; not stay with the risk-averse majority, but join 'the minority' by becoming a calculated risk-taker. This should propel you forward, with passion, enthusiasm and energy.

But even with all of this, there are things that could block this passion, enthusiasm and energy. These include your blind self, self-belief and triviality.

PART 2

BLOCKING THE PATH TO DISCOVERING INSPIRATION

"WE CANNOT
SOLVE OUR
PROBLEMS WITH
THE SAME
THINKING WE
USED WHEN WE
CREATED THEM."

Albert Einstein

CHAPTER 4
INVISIBLE BARRIERS

BLIND SELF

Even though I can sit at my desk and access millions of books from sites like Amazon, Waterstones or WHSmith, nothing beats walking into a bookshop.

As soon as I walk through the door, and I'm greeted by the aroma of coffee and that particular smell of new books, I feel a sense of calm and cosiness. I've entered a place of aspirations where the shelves are packed with ideas, wisdom, knowledge and value. I don't know why, exactly, but I love it. I tend to gravitate toward the sections where I can find books about smart thinking, business, entrepreneurship and popular psychology.

As my wife will testify, at such times I find it difficult not to buy at least one book. Sometimes I buy books that

I initially thought would be great, only to find my expectations were not met. On other occasions, I discover gems that really inspire me. And the other day I found a real gem, which is the inspiration for this chapter.

Change Your Mind: 57 Ways to Unlock your Creative Self is a book by Rod Judkins, an artist and writer who lectures at the Central St Martins College of Art in London. In it, he shares an inspiring story about 'barriers.'

Judkins was asked to teach a design class when the normal lecturer was away. He set the students the challenge of making a paper airplane from a single A4 sheet of paper that could travel at least 60 feet across the room. The students came up with a huge variety of designs and tried different methods of launching and then flying their planes.

After countless failures to launch, corkscrews and nose-dives, they became disheartened and started to believe that the goal wasn't achievable. Finally, one student became so frustrated that he scrunched his paper airplane into a ball and threw it into a trash bin on the other side of the room.

Once Judkins saw that every student had tried and failed, he got up from his desk, walked across the room to where the bin was located and took out the scrunched-up paper plane. He declared this plane the winner, as it had travelled the required distance, and congratulated the student who'd piloted the paper ball into the bin.

The students looked bewildered, and Judkins responded: "Who said airplanes had to look like airplanes?"

Judkins' challenge was all about pushing the barriers of the students' imagination. He was trying to get them to see that their thinking was inhibited because they consciously assumed there were barriers, when in fact there weren't. He wanted to inspire them to push back – to break through their deep-seated preconceptions – in order to achieve what they initially thought was impossible.

The question becomes how to push back your own invisible boundaries, which may be stopping you from finding new sources of inspiration. Well, let me share some ideas.

JOHARI HOUSE

In 1955 the American psychologists Joseph Luft and Harrington Ingham developed a model to help people better understand their relationship with themselves and others. They called it 'Johari's Window,' with the word 'Johari' deriving from a combination of their first names. In 2000, the author and philosopher Charles Handy developed a leadership and management tool based on the model, called 'Johari House,' which aimed to develop self-awareness.

Handy believed that in order to develop self-awareness, you need to be aware not only of how you see yourself, but also how others see you. The Johari House is Handy's analogy for a person, and he developed a model that can be applied to you, me or anyone, to help us become more self-aware.

Within the Johari House there are four rooms, each representing the four parts of any individual:

- **Room 1** is the part of you that both you and others see – the open self. For example, you may be incredibly organized. You focus on timelines and deadlines, you set up routines and you are disciplined. You know that, and everyone around you knows it too.

- **Room 2** is the place that contains the parts of you that only others see; you yourself are not aware of them. This is the blind self.

- In **Room 3** lies the subconscious part of you, which is seen neither by you nor others – it is the unknown self. This is the part that traditional psychologists like to talk about: Freud's area.

- **Room 4** is your private space; the part that you know but keep from others. It is the hidden self. This is the room where you keep your most intimate thoughts – the things you would not tell anyone else about.

In my view, Room 2 is the most fascinating in the Johari House, as it has the potential to block you from discovering new sources of inspiration. Fundamentally, your blind self contains aspects of your behaviour and personality that can either hold you back or propel you forward.

Here are some examples of how you could be unaware all those traits and behaviours you exhibit, which everyone else recognizes but of which you are ignorant.

BLIND SPOTS AND INVISIBLE BARRIERS

Like the students in Judkins' design class, everyone has 'blind spots' or 'invisible barriers.' These are your behaviours that you don't understand, or you fail to appreciate the impact they have on yourself or others.

In her book, *Fearless Leadership*, Dr Loretta Malandro identifies eight behavioural blind spots that can stop you from becoming the best you can be:

- **Having an 'I know' attitude.** You think that you're always right and those who disagree with you are wrong. This includes not listening to others' views, refusing to explore other options and making assumptions about others' intent or their ideas.

- **Being insensitive of your behavior toward others.** You judge others not by their intentions, but by their actions. You choose words that can be mean or misunderstood and provoke negative responses. You don't realize how your behaviour and actions actually give others a feeling of worthlessness.

- **Avoiding difficult conversations.** You always try to avoid conflict and stressful situations, and therefore avoid conversations where that can happen.

- **Going it alone.** You do things without asking others for their input because you feel like you need to get things done on your own. This can include not accepting help from others and not including others in decisions.

- **Blaming others or circumstances**. You avoid the need to take accountability or try to negate it by shifting blame. You always have a reason, excuse or explanation for why something went wrong.

- **Not sticking to commitments**. You don't keep to your obligations. You regularly show up late for meetings or don't get projects done on time. You constantly use the words 'I'll try' rather than 'I will.'

- **Conspiring against others**. You talk negatively behind people's backs, engage in gossip and spread conspiracy theories. You discredit others' ideas or accomplishments without telling them face-to-face.

- **Not taking a stand**. You know you should do something about an important issue, but you don't because of how it could impact you. You don't speak up when you're with friends or in a meeting, even though you disagree with the majority view on something.

	KNOWN TO SELF	**UNKNOWN TO SELF**
KNOWN TO OTHERS	**OPEN SELF** Information about you that both you and others know.	**BLIND SELF** Information about you that you don't know but others do know.
UNKNOWN TO OTHERS	**HIDDEN SELF** Information about you that you know but others don't know.	**UNKOWN SELF** Information about you that neither you nor others know.

MAKING ROOM 2
SMALLER

━━━━━

The following will hopefully help you gain clarity around your blind spots, understand how they affect you and learn how to manage them better. This will open the door for personal growth and learning, which in turn will make you far more self-aware in everything you do.

Find someone you really trust.

Understanding and accepting that you have blind spots is the first step. Find someone who is insightful enough to see clearly what you cannot, and who's willing to speak the truth to you. Most people either don't have the insight or don't have the courage to do this. Find that rare person who knows you well and is willing to tell you difficult information. Ask this person to talk about what they see as your bind spots, assuring them that what they say won't compromise your relationship.

Surround yourself with diverse thinkers.

Meet people who have different views, experiences or perspectives with the intention of learning from them. How do you find these people? Not everyone wants to join a business club, book club, sports club, or enrol in a course, attend a networking event or go to an art exhibition. If that's you, turn to the internet. There are so many fascinating and inspiring people you can 'meet' on Wikipedia, YouTube, blogs, Instagram, TED Talks, LinkedIn and Twitter.

Examine your past to identify patterns.
Look back on successes in your life. What behaviours did you exhibit that brought you there? Are you now embarrassed about how you might have conducted yourself, or treated people who helped lead to your success? What meaningful feedback have you received from people who are close to you, or from mentors and coaches, regarding decisions you've made?

Identify your triggers.
We all have triggers – situations that cause us to impulsively or instinctively react without thinking. In his bestselling book, *Triggers*, leadership expert Marshall Goldsmith explains that every waking moment is filled with people, events and circumstances that have the power to shape how we act or react. When we master our triggers, we master our responses and make them work for us, rather than against us.

> "YOU CAN
> FOOL YOURSELF,
> YOU KNOW.
> YOU'D THINK
> IT'S IMPOSSIBLE,
> BUT IT TURNS OUT
> IT'S THE EASIEST
> THING OF ALL."

Jodi Picoult

Accept that, like everyone else, you have blind spots – that's absolutely normal. Find someone you really trust, and surround yourself with diverse thinkers. Take the time to examine how you behaved in various situations and learn to recognize your triggers.

If you take these steps, your blind self will slowly become more aware of how you act and react when facing a wide range of challenges and circumstances. This will help you remove some of the 'invisible barriers' to finding and harnessing new sources of inspiration. In fact, it will do the opposite, as you find new sources of inspiration all around.

CHAPTER 5
FAKING IT

SELF-BELIEF

I recently listened to Tom Hanks being interviewed by Terry Gross on the American radio show *Fresh Air*, about his new film, *A Hologram for the King*. Hanks is one of my favourite actors, with both *Apollo 13* and *Toy Story* ranking way up there in my top-ten list of films.

A brilliant and lauded actor, Hanks always comes across as a friendly, genuine, relaxed person. He's starred in more than 75 films, won 2 Oscars and as of 2019 had a net worth of roughly $350 million. Hanks is ranked fifth-highest all-time box office star in North America, with films grossing over $4.9 billion there and $9.96 billion worldwide. He's been called 'America's Dad' and even had an asteroid named after him: 12818 Tomhanks.

Therefore, it would be reasonable to assume that he is confident and self-assured in his abilities as an actor. But, as the recent radio interview revealed, nothing could be further from truth.

In *A Hologram for the King*, Hanks plays a middle-aged American businessman who's sent to Saudi Arabia, where the king is planning to build a new city in the middle of the desert. Hanks' character, Adam Clay, is tasked with persuading the Saudis to let the company he works for provide IT technology and support for this new city.

Hanks said he felt particularly connected with his character's sense of self-doubt and dislocation, as they hit close to home. "No matter what we've done, there comes a point where you think, 'How did I get here? When are they going to discover that I am, in fact, a fraud and take everything away from me?'"

Despite all his achievements, Hanks still finds himself doubting his own abilities. "It's a high-wire act that we all walk," he said.

"There are days when I know that three o'clock tomorrow afternoon I am going to have to deliver some degree of emotional goods, and if I can't do it, that means I'm going to have to fake it. If I fake it, that means they might catch me at faking it, and if they catch me at faking it, well, then it's just doomsday."

I have to say, I was staggered to hear this. Here was a man full of self-doubt and dislocation, which I never would have assumed. And the interview also showed another characteristic – the actor's honesty. He was very open about feeling like a 'fraud.'

The interview resonated with me in a fundamental way. I found that I related to what Hanks was describing: that feeling of being a fraud, and fear of being 'found out.' And while I recognize that I've achieved a lot in life, it doesn't stop me from feeling like Hanks at times.

I talked to a good friend, who is a trained therapist, about all this. She told me that it's a recognized condition called Imposter Syndrome. And the more I researched it, the more I could relate to it. I also found that Hanks isn't the only famous person who suffers from it

Facebook's Sheryl Sandberg, musician David Bowie, tennis player Serena Williams, Starbucks founder Howard Schultz, civil rights activist, author, poet and Nobel Laureate Maya Angelou, *Huffington Post* founder Arianna Huffington, and musician Lady Gaga have all admitted to feeling like frauds, despite their achievements, and expecting to be found out.

Just listen to what actress Emma Watson said about this: "Now, when I receive recognition for my acting, I feel incredibly uncomfortable," she said. "I tend to turn in on myself. I feel like an imposter."

If you can relate to some or all of this, there's a good chance that these feelings are blocking you from finding and harnessing new sources of inspiration. You will need to put strategies in place to counter this self-doubt.

However, before I focus on those, let's take a closer look at Imposter Syndrome.

"I FEEL LIKE AN IMPOSTER."

Emma Watson

THE IMPOSTOR
PHENOMENON

A 2011 report, "The Impostor Phenomenon," estimated that 70% of the US population had experienced Impostor Syndrome to some degree or another.

Basically, someone harbouring these doubts will feel as though they don't belong where they are; that they only got there through luck. Sometimes, the disorder can fuel feelings of motivation to achieve, but this usually comes at a cost, such as constant anxiety. You might over-prepare, or work much harder than necessary, to make sure nobody finds out that you're faking it.

This could lead to you being stuck in an 'impostor cycle,' where success creates a continuous loop of self-doubt. Every time you accomplish something, you become more worried that others will discover the 'truth' about your abilities (or lack thereof).

In a terrible twist, the experience of doing well at something does nothing to change these people's beliefs. Even though you might sail through a pitch or deliver a brilliant speech, the nagging thought still haunts you: 'What gives me the right to be here?' The more you accomplish, the more you just feel like a fraud.

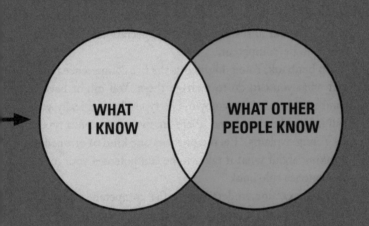

THE FIVE
IMPOSTERS

━━━━━

Decades of research by Dr Valerie Young, author of *The Secret Thoughts of Successful Women: Why Capable People Suffer from Impostor Syndrome and How to Thrive in Spite of It*, revealed that the core source of imposter feelings are the unrealistic and unsustainably high expectations for what it means to be 'competent.'

In her book, Young highlights the five competence types and what you can do to manage them. You might have a combination of these competence types, but typically you will have a dominant one. There are five competence types. As Young explains, "Each represents one kind of erroneous thinking about what it takes to be competent – your inner competence rule book."

Let's examine, in detail, these five competent types and how you manage them.

━━━━━━━━━━

- **The Perfectionist's View of Competence.**
  Perfectionists have a single focus on how something should be done. You believe in the statement, 'I should deliver 100% performance every single time I do something. Everything I do must be exemplary, where perfection is the ultimate goal.'

The downsides of being a Perfectionist is that you are likely to experience high levels of anxiety, doubt and worry, especially when you fail to achieve your extreme goals. Anything less than 'top marks' means failure. This can lead you to avoid attempting anything new or difficult. And when you take on something new, you always believe you could have done a better job. You tend to focus on areas where you could have done better rather than celebrate the things you did well.

To get through all of this, Young says you will need to reframe your current thinking about what it means to be competent. Specifically, she says you need to replace your perfectionist thinking by understanding that:

» Perfectionism inhibits success
» Sometimes good is good enough
» Not everything deserves 100%
» Your perfectionism impacts others
» Non-perfection is to be embraced

- **The Natural Genius's View of Competence.**
  The competence type Young dubs the Natural Genius believes that intelligence and ability are innate. This leads to thinking that achieving success should be effortless. You think 'the reason why I can't do this project is that I am not clever enough.' Therefore, like the Perfectionists, the Natural Genius sets the internal bar for

measuring their own success impossibly high. However, unlike the Perfectionist, here you do not judge yourself on preforming flawlessly, but rather based on the ease and speed by which you achieve something.

As Young explains, "You expect to know without being taught, to excel without effort, and to get it right on the first attempt." If you have to struggle to master something or understand, you often feel ashamed. When you start something, maybe a new project, and you find it more difficult than you envisaged you blame yourself. You think you don't have the right level of intelligence and ability, rather than trying to work out new solutions that will help you.

To help you shift your thinking about competence, Young says you need to swap your false thoughts that everything should be easy and quick with these more realistic inner rules:

    » Effort trumps ability
    » Challenges are often opportunities in disguise
    » Real success always takes time

- **The Expert's View of Competence.**
  In the Expert's mind you can never have too much knowledge or skills. You think, 'If I was really clever, I would be able to understand a chapter in a book I am reading, or a ten minute scientific podcast, but I can't.'

In the Expert's mind, Young says, there will always be one more webcast to watch, book and blog to read, or one more qualification to achieve. Then you think you will have mastered a subject. However, that never feels enough. As an expert you continuously hunt for new information and knowledge, but this prevents you from achieving your goals. You need to feel comfortable before taking on new challenges and therefore you constantly seek new facts.

Your problem, however, is you won't take on any new challenges or goals until you ascertain that you can deliver on your promises. And that means you limit yourself in the opportunities that could be incredibly rewarding.

The key, says Young, is to replace the unhealthy expectations of the Expert by recognizing:

» There are many paths to expertise
» There is no end of knowledge
» Competentcy means respecting your limitations
» You don't need to know everything, you just need someone who does
» Even when you don't know something you can still project confidence
» Even when you don't know something, you should still project confidence

- **The Soloist Individualist's View of Competence.**

  If you identify with the Soloist mindset then you mistakenly believe that asking for help will reveal your incompetence. You think, 'If I was really competent, I could do everything myself.'

  In your mind, the only achievements that really count are those you reached all on your own. You believe that if you achieve something as part of a team, then it is somehow diminished. Therefore, you 'go it alone' – a pattern that may result in overworking which can in turn damage your health and your personal relationships.

  Allow sufficient time to complete an objective, challenge or project; find that extra information that will allow you to asses a situation or proceed to the next stage; seek out people who have more information than you; accept working with others means your chances of success has increased.

  Young says the key for the Soloist is to embrace new ways of thinking about what it means to be competent. Specifically:
  - » To get the job done, you need to identify the resources required
  - » Competent people know how to ask for what they need
  - » Smart people seek out people who know more than they do

» When seeking advice, it's important to ask the right people
» Your work does not need to be ground-breaking to be good
» Competent people know that it's okay to build on the work of other competent people

- **The Superwoman/man's View of Competence.** The Superwoman/man can easily be confused with the Perfectionist. But beyond the quest to perform flawlessly, here you believe competence is measured by how much you can excel all at the same time. You think, 'If I cannot 'spin all the plates' currently I have in my life, then I must not be competent.'

  The Superwoman/man often do excel in their multiple roles at work and at home, mainly because they push themselves so hard. However, this overload of work can eventually result in burnout, which can affect physical health, mental wellbeing and relationships with others.

  This means you need to reframe your thinking to accept that it is not possible to perform at the top of you game in all areas of your life simultaneously. This will only result in failure. Instead Young says you need to see that competence is not a function of how many things you can juggle. The focus for you is to try to do less. Recognize that:

- » It's okay to say no
- » Delegating frees you up and gives others the chance to participate
- » Slowing down, reflecting and then focusing on the activities that really matter
- » Being a Superwoman/man sends an unhealthy message to your daughters and sons

---

If you want to give yourself the best chance to find and harness new sources of inspiration, then you need to redefine what it means to be competent in the challenges and goals you take on. Remember that luck has indeed played a part in what you've achieved so far. (We'll explore the importance of luck in Chapter 14.) That does not make you a fraud.

Whatever success you've achieved is also attributable to your hard work, talent and commitment. Yes, like everyone, you've gotten some 'breaks' along the way. Good for you! That doesn't make you a phony.

The point is simply to start accepting and embracing what you have achieved so far in your life. Be grateful and feel inspired to build on that success.

CHAPTER 6
THE FOCUSING ILLUSION

TRIVIALITY

Warren Buffett, the investor, philanthropist and third-richest person in the world, lives a very modest lifestyle, despite his net worth of around $85 billion.

Buffett, chairman of the multinational conglomerate Berkshire Hathaway, pulls an annual salary of $100,000, which hasn't changed in more than a quarter-century. He bought a five-bedroom house in Omaha, Nebraska, for $31,500 in 1958 and has lived there ever since. He's known for his simple tastes (McDonald's hamburgers and Cherry Coke) and his disdain for technology (no cell phone or desktop computer).

Although he could afford a fleet of limousines, he prefers to drive himself in his six-year-old Cadillac XTS sedan.

When it comes to entertainment, he prefers playing a quiet game of bridge over attending splashy parties.

In 1998, Buffett gave a lecture to students at the University of Florida School of Business. He laid out a scenario to illustrate why they should be satisfied with their lives, and not be fooled into the trap of wishing for a different life with 'better' material goods.

He told his audience to imagine a barrel filled with roughly 5.8 billion balls – one for each person in the world. He explained that each individual's ball determined important factors, including their parents, birthplace, IQ level, gender, ethnicity and skills.

"If you could put your ball [current life] back into the barrel, and they took out 100 balls at random – and you had to pick from one of those – would you put your ball back in?" he asked.

In addition to not knowing which ball you'll get – and what sort of 'new life' it would drop you into – there was another catch. "Of those 100 balls," Buffett explained, "five of them will be American. So, if you want to be in this country, you'll only have five balls to choose from. Half of them will be women and half men. Half of them will be below average in intelligence and half above average in intelligence."

He asked the students again: Do you still want to risk taking a second shot at life?

"Most of you won't want to put your ball back," he said. "So, what you're really saying is this, 'I'm the luckiest 1% of the world right now, sitting in this room — the top 1% of the world.'"

"NOTHING IN LIFE IS
AS IMPORTANT AS
YOU THINK IT IS
WHILE YOU ARE
THINKING ABOUT IT."

Daniel Kahneman

———

He closed the lecture by encouraging everyone to think about happiness from a more practical standpoint. None of us can live life all over again, he suggested, but we can increase our overall happiness by choosing to make changes in our career, goals, finances, health and relationships.

"The way to do it is to play out the game and do something you'll enjoy all your life," he said. "Be associated with people you like. I only work with people I like. If I could make $100 million with a guy who causes my stomach to churn, I'd say no."

He continued: "I urge you to work in jobs you love. You're out of your mind if you keep taking jobs that you don't like because you think it'll look good on your resume."

How many times have you asked yourself how much better life would be if you had a different job, or lived in a different location, had a different house and drove a different car? I accept that it might make some people happier in the short term, but you need to put everything into perspective.

A great analogy to help you do this is to imagine that you're viewing your life through a camera lens. Remember that different types of lenses make things look different. A narrow-angle lens makes things appear closer together, and you will only be focusing in on a few of them. A wide-angle lens gets more things in the shot, allowing you to see far more.

Try and see your life in that way. Don't focus on a few things you might think will make you happy, but take the longest view of your life. By doing this you'll realize that what once seemed so important for your happiness has become irrelevant when compared to other rewarding and satisfying things you could be putting your energy into.

Finding and harnessing sources of inspiration that can translate into success is about trying to see life through the 'wide-angle lens.'

DOES MONEY BUY HAPPINESS?

You probably assume that multi-millionaires, with their yachts, exotic holidays and luxurious estates, are supremely happy. However, that's not necessarily the case.

The American psychologist, economist and author Daniel Kahneman was part of team from Princeton University that studied whether money really did make people happier. They found that those with high incomes are more likely than others to say that they're happy with their lives, but this difference generally disappears when they make a moment-to-moment assessment of how happy they really are.

The study, entitled "Would You Be Happier If You Were Richer? A Focusing Illusion," and published in *Science* magazine, found that people are deluded into believing that more money will invariably make them happier. They described a phenomenon – 'focusing illusion' – whereby the more narrowly an individual focuses on a particular aspect of their lives, the greater its apparent influence.

"When people consider the impact of any single factor on their wellbeing – not only income – they are prone to exaggerate its importance," they wrote.

So, when survey respondents are asked whether wealthier people are happier than the less well-off, they tend to focus on financial status as the root of happiness. Perhaps seduced by thoughts of plasma TVs and seaside resorts, they make too much of the effect wealth can have on one's wellbeing.

In reality, according to the study, higher income does little to improve life satisfaction, and may even cause more anxiety and stress. "In some cases," explained the authors, "this focusing illusion may lead to a misallocation of time, from accepting lengthy commutes to sacrificing time spent socializing."

Indeed, in the results of a national survey the authors analysed, people with an income above $100,000 reported spending more time than others at work and commuting. This may help to explain why so many people with relatively high incomes reported that they're generally happy with their lives, but don't actually experience as much happiness as they say they do. "People do not know how happy or satisfied they are with their life in the way they know their height or telephone number," the researchers reported.

Overcoming the focusing illusion is key to helping you discover meaningful success. It will enable you to avoid making stupid decisions. When you compare things like cars, careers and holiday destinations, you tend to focus on one aspect of your life particularly closely, neglecting the hundreds of other factors. You assign this one piece inordinate significance because of the focusing illusion.

In his book, *The Art of The Good Life*, the Swiss businessman Rolf Dobelli describes another study that Kahnmenan carried out with University of Michigan psychologists Norbert Schwartz and Jing Xu.

The researchers asked motorists how much pleasure, on a scale of 0–10, they get from their car. They then compared the responses with the monetary value of the vehicles. The results showed that the more luxurious the car, the more pleasure it gave the owner. For instance, a BMW 7 Series generates about 50% more pleasure than a Ford Escort. Their conclusion: when somebody sinks a load of money into a car, at least they get a good return on their investment in the form of joy.

But there was an interesting twist. The researchers also asked, "How happy were you during your last car trip?" They then compared the motorists' answers with the values of their cars. Surprisingly, there was absolutely no correlation. Whether they were driving a top-end luxury sedan or a second-hand banger, there was no apparent connection between the vehicle and how happy they were feeling out on the highway.

Question one showed a definite correlation between the perceived pleasure a car gave its owner and its monetary value. Yet, the second question revealed no correlation at all – a luxury car didn't make the drivers any happier out on the road. You see, the first question makes you think solely about the car, while the second directs you to think of other things that happen while you're driving, like fretting that you'll be late for a meeting, receiving a hostile phone call or getting stuck in a traffic jam.

That is the effect of the focusing illusion – a car makes you happy when you're thinking about it, but not when you're driving it. Thinking about your purchase of the car abstractly makes you happy, but the more you actually use it, this fades to the back of your mind and that minimizes the effect on your happiness.

ENRICHING
YOUR LIFE

Think about other purchases you've made. If you are a homeowner, think back to when you bought your house. The initial delight of having your offer accepted, closing on the deal and moving in gradually wanes as daily management of the house takes over. For example, there are costly expenditures that come with mending the roof, painting the rooms and sorting out the garden. You may find yourself dwelling on the inconvenience of the location or a loud neighbour.

As with driving your car, there is a net loss of happiness when you really examine the purchase and think about it. We go through the same exercise with technology purchases, holiday homes, etc.

All of these things can distract you from finding and harnessing sources of inspiration. How can you spend your time doing things that enrich and benefit your life when your thoughts are consumed by purchasing material goods?

All too often, we're conned into the illusion that this stuff will make us happy, but all the evidence shows that it actually doesn't.

Everyone overestimates the impact of material purchases on their wellbeing and underestimates the impact of experiences. We don't fully appreciate experiences like watching a great film, reading a good book, going out for dinner with your family or going on a long walk with your dogs. Yes, some experiences require money, but these routine, feel-good activities are far better investments as sources of inspiration and meaning in your life.

Let's go back to Warren Buffett. His modest lifestyle shows that he figured out a long time ago that material luxuries do not increase happiness. He recommends not wasting your time wishing life was different or wanting material things. Rather, he suggests pursuing things that give you genuine satisfaction and long-term contentment.

To find and harness sources of inspiration that translate into success, you need to: remove the invisible barriers you've created as you discover more about your blind self; identify what 'imposter' you think you are and start to remove that belief from your life, accepting that you are not a phoney; view your life through the widest-angle lens; focus far less on material goods and more on having experiences.

And then, with this uncluttered foundation in place and the blocks on the path removed, there are many fascinating ways to discover and harness sources of inspiration that can lead to meaningful and rewarding success.

PART 3

IDEAS THAT LEAD TO THE SOURCES OF INSPIRATION

> "TWO ROADS DIVERGED IN A WOOD, AND I – I TOOK THE ONE LESS TRAVELLED BY, AND THAT HAS MADE ALL THE DIFFERENCE."

Robert Frost

CHAPTER 7
BRILLIANT HANNAH
LEADING WITH PURPOSE

Sometimes you meet someone for the first time, and you think, 'Wow, what an inspiration!'

Wow, because of what they have been through and had to cope with, both physically and emotionally. Wow that they are not bitter about the 'cards' that life has dealt them. Wow, because all of this is not going to stop them from having big dreams, ambitions and goals. And then WOW, because they've turned these dreams and ambitions into reality.

Let me introduce you to an extraordinary young woman, whose life has inspired me greatly. She's 16-year-old Hannah Pierce. Hannah was born with cerebral palsy, a neurological disorder that affects movement, posture, speech and coordination. Since the age of four, she has either been in a wheelchair or on an adapted bed.

I was introduced to Hannah by a mutual friend, who suggested that I might be able to help her with a digital project – an online magazine she was working on. The moment she arrived in the coffee shop in her motorized wheelchair, her energy and positivity were immediately evident.

Hannah is the founder of *Communitea*, an online magazine aimed at helping people see the world differently. It features contributions from individuals living with disabilities, and those working with and supporting them. Hannah was inspired to start *Communitea* because she never saw a version of herself portrayed in the media.

Her mission is simple but powerful: to create a space where people with disabilities are included, never feel alone and can support each other, through online forums and shared stories. Through great, compelling content, she hopes to fight the stigma surrounding the disabled. She wants to make this community as big and as inclusive as possible, with participants from around the globe. She has already raised financing and the website is now live.

She passionately explains that she wants *Communitea* to change peoples' lives, as much as it has changed hers. And, she says, this is only the beginning; she has even more ambitious plans. Having spent time with Hannah, I would not bet against her achieving these dreams. What really struck me at our first meeting was her passion for ensuring that those with disabilities get equality.

Discovering new things and ideas that you can genuinely care about – and feel downright passionate about – is one route to inspired thinking. When you find these things, make them the centre of your daily life. You will feel energized, motivated and excited, which will lead you to meaningful success. Hannah demonstrates this perfectly.

DEVELOPING, NOT FINDING, YOUR PASSION

However, finding something that you're passionate about and sticking with it is not as simple as it sounds. Carol Dweck, Professor of Psychology at Stanford University, once asked an undergraduate seminar, "How many of you are waiting to find your passion?"

And this is the response she got, according to Olga Khazan, a staff writer at *The Atlantic*, who interviewed her: "Almost all of them raised their hand and got dreamy looks in their eyes," she said. "They talked about it like a tidal wave would sweep over them."

Would they have unlimited motivation for their passion? They nodded solemnly. "I hate to burst your balloon," Dweck told them, "but it doesn't usually happen that way."

What Dweck was examining is the commonly-used mantra, 'Follow your passion.' I have to admit that, in the past,

I've been guilty of telling people that if they want happiness and contentment, they need to find the things they are passionate about.

But, according to Dweck's research and others, it's all more complicated than that.

Paul O'Keefe, an Assistant Professor of Psychology at Yale University, told Khazan that urging people to find their passion can cause problems. "What are the consequences of that?" he asked. "That means that if you do something that feels like work, it means you don't love it." He gave the example of a student who jumps from lab to lab, trying to find one whose research topic feels like her passion. "It's this idea that if I'm not completely overwhelmed by emotion when I walk into a lab, then it won't be my passion or my interest."

O'Keefe, along with Dweck and Greg Walton, an Associate Professor of Psychology at Stanford University, published a study on O'Keefe's website, *Mindsets and Motivation Lab*. Their report – "Implicit Theories of Interest: Finding your passion or developing it?" – suggested that passions aren't simply stumbled upon, they can also be developed.

They explain that there are two types of mindsets that can determine what you will pursue as a career. One is a 'fixed theory of interests,' the idea that core interests are there from birth, just waiting to be discovered. The other is a 'growth theory,' the idea that interests are something anyone can cultivate over time.

The researchers performed a series of studies on college students, a group that's frequently advised to find their passion in the form of a career path. Their study showed that students who have fixed theories of interest might forgo interesting lectures or promising opportunities because they don't align with what they previously thought they were passionate about. Those with a growth theory of interests were far more open to new ideas and opportunities.

Another downside of having a fixed theory mindset is that it can cause people to give up too easily. If something becomes difficult, it's easy to assume that it simply must not have been your passion, after all. In one portion of this study, the students with fixed theory mindsets were also less likely to think that pursuing a passion would be difficult at times. They thought it would provide 'endless motivation.'

So, the good news from all of this is that if you haven't yet found your passion, don't worry. If, on the other hand, you've already stumbled upon it, and think you just need to start developing it further, I'd suggest that you need to approach this in a slightly different way.

> ## "THE PERSON WITHOUT A PURPOSE IS LIKE A SHIP WITHOUT A RUDDER."

Thomas Carlyle

START WITH
YOUR PURPOSE –
PASSION WILL FOLLOW

People normally think that purpose and passion are roughly the same. Actually, they're fundamentally different.

Purpose is the reason, the 'why' question behind what drives us in life. ('What contribution am I making to my own life and the lives of others?') Passion is about emotions, the things that inspire you, motivate you and make you feel good. ('Do what you love!')

Purpose tends to be more outwardly focused, as it generally has an impact on not only yourself but on others. Being passionate about something tends to be inwardly focused, making you excited and motivated in the short term. Getting passionate about something tends to come and go, whereas purpose tends to be longer term and more focused.

Achieving meaningful and rewarding success is when you figure out a way to align your purpose and your passions.

Let's go back to the question that Dweck asked the undergraduate seminar: "How many of you are waiting to find your passion?" I would love to have asked, "How many of you are waiting to find your purpose?"

In my previous book, *Positive Thinking: How to Create a World Full of Possibilities*, I dedicate a whole chapter to 'purpose' and why it's so important to identify your purpose. Your purpose provides you with a stable foundation and a sense of direction, both of which are integral to a positive outlook on life. Purpose can guide life decisions, influence behaviour, shape goals and create meaning.

However, there's more to discovering your purpose than aligning it with your passion (the things that you love to do). You also need to align it with your mission (the things that you're good at), your profession (which earns you an income), and also your strengths (the things you do that seem natural to you).

Going back to young Hannah Pierce, she perfectly embodies the notion of finding and living with a strong purpose.

Hannah's purpose is to create a space where people with disabilities will be included, support each other and never feel alone, through visibility, forums and shared stories. One of the ways she's done this was by creating *Communitea*. She's passionate about her online magazine, and wants it to change people's lives as much as it has changed hers.

Hannah has received grants and sponsorship for the magazine, and this is now her profession. She's been working with a web designer to create and manage *Communitea*, and she and others write and publish articles there. This is her mission. To achieve all of this, and overcome the daily challenges she faces, she is absolutely using her strengths much of the time. What she's achieving seems natural to her, as it is helping not only herself, but countless others who live with a disability.

And that is why Hannah has found real and meaningful purpose in her life. Take a leaf out of Hannah's book and discover the ideas and sources that will inspire you to answer the 'why' question – your purpose – in what you want to achieve. This will help inspire you to identify your mission, profession, strengths and passion. And that will ultimately lead you to meaningful success… which is precisely what Hannah is achieving.

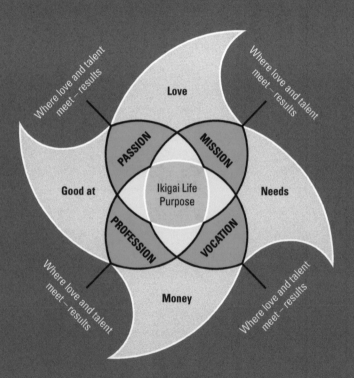

Source: ©RubixPotential

CHAPTER 8
SPIRIT OF ADVENTURE
STAYING YOUNG

In *Positive Thinking*, I shared a story about my good friends Steve and Lynda Dalgleish. About six years ago, Steve and his wife Lynda went on a sailing holiday in the Mediterranean. They both loved the experience, but for Steve it was the catalyst for a dream that one day they would buy a catamaran and sail around the world.

At that time, his dream was not possible for several reasons. The first and most obvious was that Steve did not know how to sail. Second, they weren't in a financial position to buy a catamaran. Third, Steve had recently been diagnosed with a heart condition that would require regular check-ups. And finally, Lynda did not share her husband's dream!

However, they found solutions to these four obstacles and left the UK in March 2019, six months after they'd both retired, and set sail across the Mediterranean. As I write this, in December of 2019, they've so far sailed to parts of Spain, Italy, Greece and Gibraltar, and have now arrived in the Caribbean.

I find what they're doing incredibly inspiring because they made the dream a reality. My guess is that the majority of people who get to retirement age tend to choose a 'safer' lifestyle and do far less adventurous things. But, as Steve and Lynda so perfectly demonstrate, there are exceptions.

In an article in *The Times*, "Our Spirit of Adventure Lives For Ever," journalist Libby Purves wrote about a remarkable man named Tony Curphey. The 74-year-old former truck driver had just returned to the UK in his 32-foot boat, the Nicola Deux, after sailing solo, non-stop, around the world. He'd been the oldest person to compete in the Golden Globe Race, which set off in June of 2018. He navigated 30,000 miles in 308 days, drinking rainwater – sometimes living on nothing but four cups of water a day – and surviving violent storms and 50-foot waves.

During his ten months alone at sea, Curphey rounded South Africa's treacherous Cape of Good Hope, skirted Australia and New Zealand, and made a transatlantic crossing via the Azores to get back to his home in Emsworth, Hampshire.

Twenty boats set off in this revival of the classic Golden Globe race of 50 years ago, and the intrepid Curphey's was the only British craft to finish, the smallest, and the one with the lowest budget.

As Purves rightly concluded, young adventurers raise our spirits, but there is something particularly inspiring about septuagenarians who sail long distances alone. Curphey chose to do it the hard way, sailing through the Southern Ocean where the dangers are significant, the waters and winds are terrifying and even bigger ships with stronger crews can be wrecked.

I am inspired in so many ways by Curphey's, and Steve and Lynda's, adventures. They're trying something different; they take risks and have failures; their mindset is focused on how to achieve their goals; they are positive and optimistic. And, something else strikes me. At heart, I believe they feel younger than they actually are.

I asked Steve about this with the following question: How old do you feel? a) Older than you actually are; b) About the same as your actual age; c) Younger than your actual age.

His response: "I have the body of a 60-year-old and the mindset of a teenager!"

This is great news for everyone who feels younger than they actually are: there's growing evidence that this youthful feeling might really pay off, big time.

> "WE DON'T STOP PLAYING BECAUSE WE GROW OLD; WE GROW OLD BECAUSE WE STOP PLAYING."
>
> **George Bernard Shaw**

YOU'RE AS YOUNG
AS YOU FEEL

In 2015, two researchers at University College London published a study that found that older people who felt three or more years younger than their chronological age had a lower death rate than those who felt their age, or those who felt more than one year older than their actual age.

The researchers asked 6,500 men and women aged 52 and over this question: "How old do you feel you are?" The responses were as follows:

- About 70% felt three or more years younger than their actual age
- 25% felt close to their actual age
- 5% felt more than one year older than their actual age

What came next was the really interesting part. Eight years after that original study, the researchers found out which participants were still alive:

- 75% of those who had felt older than their age (25% had died)
- 82% of those who had felt their actual age (18% had died)
- 86% of those who felt younger than their actual age (14% had died)

Backing up this research is another study from The University of Virginia, which showed that once people pass the pivotal age of 25, they typically rate their subjective age as younger than their chronological age. And, the study showed, this discrepancy grows as we get older. For every decade that passes, people tend to feel that they have only gained five or six years.

It turns out that this phenomenon may have rather important implications. Recent research in this area has revealed that the extent to which people feel younger than they are is strongly associated with a whole range of positive health outcomes. People with a younger subjective age are less likely to suffer from diabetes, hypertension, depression, cognitive impairment and dementia. They also tend to report better sleep and stronger memory function.

So, how do you start feeling and thinking younger than your actual age? That's an important question, because if you make this change, it will lead you to discover new sources of inspiration that will translate into meaningful and rewarding success.

GROW YOUNGER
EACH DAY

——

Here are a few suggestions to help you feel younger than you actually are. You don't have to act on them all; just select the ones that appeal to you. The results could be life-changing.

- **Get some fresh air.**
  Researchers from the University of East Anglia in the UK were looking for an easy yet effective way to get people to exercise. It turns out that simply telling people that exercise is good for them doesn't work all that well. They analysed 42 studies on the subject across 14 countries and found that people who were part of walking groups showed significantly lower blood pressure, resting heart rate, body fat, cholesterol levels and even depression scores, compared with their levels before they embarked on group walks. They also had better lung capacity – a good indicator of fitness – and were able to walk farther.

So, you don't need to run a marathon or hit the treadmill (although these are good things to do). Just get out to your nearest park, woods or beach and have a walk with a good friend.

- **Accept life for what it is.**
  Harvard University researchers have discovered that developing a thick skin and resilience toward life's challenges and difficulties can help you feel younger than your age. Not only does resilience help you feel younger, but all the evidence shows you'll be far more energized, driven and more curious and open to new experiences.

- **Sing Sing Sing.**
  You might think you're tone deaf, but US researchers have found that the effects of singing are too good to keep your mouth shut. They're not sure why singing keeps you younger, but whether it's breathing better or simply the social togetherness of joining a choir, feeling younger is a great side effect. Singing also helps people with depression and reduces loneliness, leaving us feeling relaxed, happy and connected. Do a quick search online and find a choir in your area to join.

- **Get a dog.**
  Dogs give unconditional love and it is extremely hard to not love them back. The act of spending

time with an animal who adores you and wants to have fun with you improves your emotional wellbeing. Research also shows that the simple act of walking your dog will boost your fitness level, increase social activity and enhance your sense of wellbeing. All of these factors play a part in making you feel and think younger.

- **Learn a language.**
  If you've spent your whole life dreaming of being bilingual, now is the time to learn. A 2013 study published in the journal *Neurology* found that individuals who spoke two languages developed dementia an average of four and a half years later than people who only spoke one language. Experts say that the earlier you learn, the better… but it's never too late to learn.

- **Hit the sack.**
  If you want to feel younger, don't buy into the idea that you can burn the candle at both ends and 'sleep when you're dead.' Sleep is crucial for your body and brain functions. Contrary to popular belief, sleep experts have discovered that you don't need less sleep as you age. Apparently, you'll always need as much sleep as you can get, especially if you want to feel younger. Expert advice is to try and get a good eight hours of sleep as often as you can.

So, hopefully these ideas will show that you don't need to sail the world to feel younger. Listen to the research, act on some of these ideas, and you'll feel more energised, healthy and inspired.

The younger and more energetic you feel, the more driven you will be. This, in turn, will make you more proactive, and the benefits of that cannot be underestimated.

CHAPTER 9
RUNNING NICK

GETTING PROACTIVE

When I turned 40, I thought I should tick off one of the items on my bucket list and try and run a marathon.

I enthusiastically started training, initially running a couple of miles, building up to three and eventually getting to six miles. At this point I started to realize that this was going to be a lot harder than I'd thought. So, to quote from Stephen Covey's *The 7 Habits of Effective People*, I concluded that I would "start with the end in mind."

I jumped into my car one morning and drove 26.4 miles (the full marathon distance) from my house. I was staggered to see how far it actually was. I'd driven well past my office in Edinburgh – which some days can take me over an hour to reach by car – before I'd completed the distance.

And so, having convinced myself that I could never run a marathon, I gave up.

Fourteen years on from that failure, I was astounded to see on the news the remarkable achievement of a former banker from Dorset, in southwest England, named Nick Butter. He became the first person to run a marathon in literally *every country*. And, incredibly, he did them in sequence, back to back.

I'd made it through six excruciating miles. Butter completed marathons in 196 countries, spanning 675 days, to raise funds for the charity Prostate Cancer UK.

In January of 2018, he left his job and set out to cover 5,130 miles, taking 5.1 million steps and burning 1.5 million calories. He took 201 flights, 45 train journeys, 15 buses and 280 taxis, travelling 13,500 miles between runs. Along the way, he was hit by a car and broke his elbow, was shot at in Nigeria, got attacked by wild dogs in Tunisia and crossed battlefields in Syria. He started out in Toronto and the last countries on his itinerary were Yemen, Syria, Portugal, Cape Verde, Israel and Greece.

Butter embarked on this solo expedition after being inspired by his friend, Kevin, who had terminal cancer. In a television interview he said: "I couldn't believe that this guy, who always seemed so happy and full of life, had just told me he had terminal cancer. I was shocked, and when Kevin told me, 'Don't wait for the diagnosis,' it really struck a chord with me, and I just knew I had to do something to raise money for the charity. Kevin changed my life that day, and, in the months that followed, I quit my job at the bank and swapped my suit for running shorts, forever."

And then he said something that had a big impact on me: "The average human lives for 29,747 days, and if you're British, you spend about nine years watching television, so it's interesting to get people thinking about how much time you waste not doing something you're truly passionate about."

To me, that statement is all about proactivity. A proactive approach focuses on eliminating problems before they have a chance to take root, and grabbing the right possibilities as you're presented with them. If you're proactive, you make things happen instead of waiting for them to happen to you.

Being proactive will mean that you cannot help but discover new sources of inspiration. Over the next few pages, then, are some ideas to move you in the direction of becoming more proactive.

> ## "THE WAY TO GET STARTED IS TO QUIT TALKING AND BEGIN DOING."
>
> **Walt Disney**

ALWAYS BE READY FOR WHEN YOUR BRAIN WANTS TO TALK

———

The brain is a funny organ. If you try and force it to come up with a solution to a problem, it won't necessarily play ball. The brain decides when it will give you an inspirational thought. It could be on the train going to work, in the gym, walking the dogs or in the middle of the night. Whenever it is, you need to be ready to 'catch' that inspirational thought.

If you're looking for inspiration for your next project or venture, get into the habit of carrying a notebook and a pen. If that sounds too old school, download one of the many digital notebooks that are available. You'll then be ready to record the thought when your brain decides, without warning, to say something like, 'Hey, that newspaper article you just read could form the basis for the next chapter in the book you're writing.' Or, 'Hey, maybe the main example used in that TED talk you just watched could be worked into the presentation you're struggling to finish.'

Artist David Hockney had all the inside pockets of his suit jackets altered to fit a sketchbook. The entrepreneur Richard Branson has a habit of carrying a notebook everywhere he goes. Beethoven always carried musical score books with him, so he could jot down themes. The musician

Arthur Russell liked to wear shirts with two front pockets so he could fill them with scraps of score sheets.

Aristotle Onassis, the legendary Greek shipping tycoon, gave this advice: "Always carry a notebook. Write everything down. When you have an idea, write it down. Writing it down will make you act upon it. If you don't write it down, you will forget it."

Develop an 'addiction' to always writing down your thoughts, insights and ideas. See this notebook as a place for 'dumping' the things your brain says to you, wherever you are. As soon as it talks to you with an inspirational thought, write it down.

Be proactive and you'll be amazed how many full notebooks you end up with.

TRAVEL, TRAVEL, TRAVEL

Creative geniuses from all fields seem all too aware of how indispensable travel is to their work, boosting their creativity by inspiring and changing their thinking. Travel dishes up the inspiration to make discoveries that have defined their lives – and careers. For most, creativity and inspiration come through new and exciting experiences. But when the most exciting thing about your day is the commute to and from work, or office gossip at the water cooler, you're limiting your mind's ability to expand and be inspired.

I'm convinced that travelling is one the best ways to find inspiration. Writers and thinkers have long felt the creative benefits of international travel. Ernest Hemingway's work was heavily influenced by his time spent in France, Spain, Africa and Cuba, and Mark Twain's journey around the Mediterranean is documented in his humorous travelogue, *Innocents Abroad*. Paul Thoroux built a literary career on his travels abroad. And the philosopher Alain De Botton's wonderful The *Art of Travel* was inspired by… yes, you guessed it.

Their exposure to new and different cultures enabled these authors, and so many others, to produce some of their best work.

The physical act of travelling outside of your normal setting and everyday routine has been known to inspire breakthrough thinking. In the 1940s, on a Greyhound bus lumbering across the wheat fields of Kansas in the middle of the night, Princeton physics researcher Freeman Dyson cracked the problem of quantum electrodynamics – the theory of how radiation and atoms interact. Others had been trying to solve it for years.

Travelling helps to open your mind. You can try local foods, visit notable landmarks, make friends with new people, or even just go for a walk on a beach, through a forest or up a hill. When you're on holiday, rather than spending the whole week lying next to a pool, take at least one day and visit somewhere new. If you are attending a conference or a seminar, plan your trip to allow at least half a day to sightsee.

Simply immersing yourself in a different location for several days can inspire your creativity, help with your problem-solving and give you space to think in a different way. But you don't need to go to Rome, Bangkok or New York to be inspired by a new location. My guess is that there will be villages, towns and attractions no more than an hour from your house that you've never visited. So, jump into the car, climb onto your bike or take the bus, and go and visit them.

Just travel – you'll be amazed by how inspired your thoughts will become.

STOP TALKING
AND BEGIN DOING

The more things you're involved in, the more likely you are to chance upon that person or place – or that book, painting or cello solo – that gives you an inspirational thought, insight or idea.

Take Walt Disney, for example. He was a remarkably creative entrepreneur, animator, voice actor and film producer. He was the recipient of 22 Academy Awards and was nominated 59 times for producing iconic cartoons and animated films that we all enjoy to this day.

The more films Disney made, the more creative he became. The more creative he became, the more success he achieved. There were also some significant failures, but each time he failed, he learned his lesson and tried again. So, he just did *a lot of stuff,* with some of it ending in failure but most leading to extraordinary success. The successes included 100 feature films, the Disney television programmes and channel, and the genre-defining amusement parks, Disneyland and Disney World. The more he did, the more inspired he became to take on new projects.

Mark Twain, the famous American author, wrote dozens of novels, shorts stories, essays and articles. His most famous works are *The Adventures of Tom Sawyer* (1876) and its sequel, *The Adventures of Huckleberry Finn* (1884).

Twain said this about 'just doing': "The secret of getting ahead is getting started. The secret of getting started is breaking your complex overwhelming tasks into small management tasks, and then starting on the first one. Once you start doing, rather than procrastinating, you will find inspiration all around you."

FIND THE PERFECT
ENVIRONMENT

It's no coincidence that authors and artists find that new and different environments often give them inspiration for their next book or painting.

Likewise, companies organize 'team days' away from the office, normally in hotels or unusual venues. The very fact that employees are away from the boring routines and mundane distractions of the workplace helps them to come up with new ideas, solutions and strategies.

JK Rowling wrote most of *Harry Potter and The Philosopher's Stone* at The Elephant House Café in Edinburgh, not at her flat. Benny and Bjorn of the group ABBA would spend weeks in a mountainside hut working on new songs. London's Abbey Road Studios seems to bring out the best in musicians who use it – the Beatles produced their finest work there, as have a string of diverse, creative powerhouses such as Oasis, Ella Fitzgerald, Duran Duran, Amy Winehouse, Ed Sheeran, Radiohead, Elvis Costello and Nigel Kennedy.

Going to a specific space can allow you to disconnect from outside distractions and become totally focused and immersed, driving creative thinking.

It is important to find the right working environment to encourage creativity. Find the right environment and you'll create the ambiance that will help inspire you to be creative in whatever you're trying to achieve. And when I say creative, I mean it in its widest definition. It might be creativity in how you approach a new idea you have, an opportunity you've been presented with or a challenge you're struggling with.

If where you work gives you joy and pleasure, you are more likely to find inspiration to produce great work. The setting does not have to be huge, luxurious or exotic – it is the atmosphere and ambience that counts.

ALWAYS GO ON
YOUR GUT FEELING

When you're suddenly inspired by a thought or idea, always go along with your intuition. This is the old notion of 'going with your gut feeling,' following through on 'a hunch' or receiving 'a flash of insight.' Whatever you call it, see it for what it is – a very powerful tool.

Trust in your intuition and listen to what it's telling (or screaming out to) you. Even some of the most logical thinkers of all time made their greatest discoveries based on flashes of intuition. Think of Sir Isaac Newton and the apple that fell on his head, or the ancient Greek mathematician Archimedes shouting "Eureka!" in his bathtub. And remember what Einstein said: "The only really valuable thing is intuition."

When you're pondering whether to act on an inspirational thought, you really need to trust in what's already present and available within you: your own natural homing device, your internal GPS system – your intuition.

It's usually right. Steve Jobs famously said, "Don't let the noise of others' opinions drown out your own inner voice. And most importantly, have the courage to follow your heart and intuition." I wholeheartedly agree.

Remember, there are always new sources of inspiration around you. You just need to be prepared to actively seek them out.

CHAPTER 10
THE ROWING MARINE

BEING DETERMINED

Sometimes you read an article or hear an interview and you're truly inspired by someone else's achievement. That's what happened to me this morning.

On the BBC news, I watched in complete awe as Lee Spencer finished crossing the Atlantic from mainland Europe to South America, in a rowboat, in only 60 days. What's so remarkable about Spencer's achievement is that he's the first single-leg amputee to have rowed solo across the Atlantic. He smashed the previous able-bodied record, set by Stein Hoff in 2002, by over a month, gaining two new world records.

It took Spencer 60 days, 16 hours and 6 minutes to row from Portugal to French Guiana, where he made landfall on 11 March 2019. He had rowed unsupported for an astounding 3,500 miles.

He faced waves of up to 40 feet high, four 15-metre sperm whales swimming beneath him, being pursued by a large shark, a bout of gastroenteritis and various technical issues. He slept for just two hours at a time, all while battling the daily routine at sea and the challenges of being an amputee.

Spencer is a former Royal Marine who'd served in the armed forces for 24 years. In 2014 he lost his right leg after being hit by flying debris as he helped a motorist who'd crashed on southeast England's M3 motorway.

When asked in a BBC interview why he'd set himself the transatlantic challenge, he explained that he wanted to prove that "no one should be defined by disability."

He told BBC Radio 4's *Today* programme that he "didn't get much sleep," but added, "I have done 24 years as a Royal Marine, so I am quite used to hardship."

Moving around the unstable, tiny boat with one leg was "quite difficult," he said, but that was the whole point. "If I can beat a record, an able-bodied record, as a disabled man… that is the reason why I wanted to do this. To prove that no one should be defined by their disability."

Spencer's inspiring story is about many things, including courage, commitment, perseverance and bravery, but above all else it's a story of determination.

"THE MAN WHO
CAN DRIVE HIMSELF
FURTHER ONCE
THE EFFORT GETS
PAINFUL IS THE MAN
WHO WILL WIN."

Roger Bannister

NINE THINGS THE 'DETERMINED' DO

If you've got a major goal – like setting up your own business, taking on a physical challenge or learning a new language – you'll never get there without a serious dose of determination! Determination is to success what oxygen is to life. It is a prerequisite.

By trying to understand the behaviours and characteristics of determined people, you can learn how to use determination to take on new possibilities and opportunities, and succeed at them. For example, when you're training for a marathon and the wind is in your face, the rain is pouring down and you are cold and sore, but you still stick to the route you were planning to cover, that determination will inspire and help you the next time you go for a run.

Anyone who has ever achieved anything significant has done so on the back of their determination. The good news is that, regardless of how much grit and conviction you have shown to date, you can still increase your levels of determination.

Let's look at what I think are the main nine behaviours and characteristics of 'the determined.'

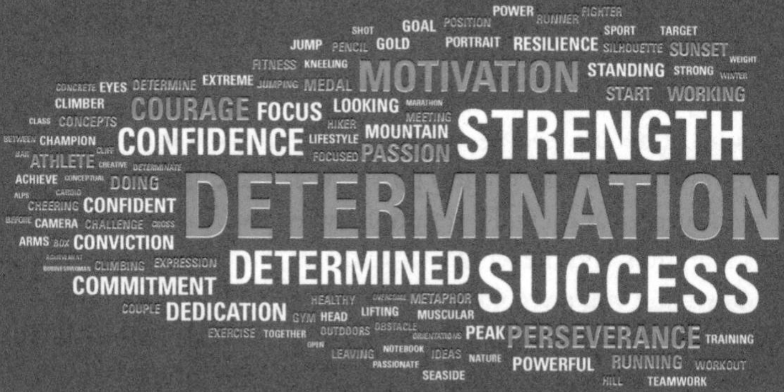

POWER
RUNNER
FIGHTER
SHOT
GOAL
POSITION
SPORT
TARGET
JUMP
PENCIL
GOLD
PORTRAIT
RESILIENCE
SILHOUETTE
SUNSET
WEIGHT
FITNESS
KNEELING
MOTIVATION
STANDING
STRONG
WINTER
CONCRETE
EYES
DETERMINE
EXTREME
JUMPING
MEDAL
START
WORKING
CLIMBER
COURAGE
FOCUS
LOOKING
MARATHON
MEETING
CLASS
CONCEPTS
HIKER
STRENGTH
BETWEEN
CHAMPION
CONFIDENCE
LIFESTYLE
MOUNTAIN
BAR
ATHLETE
CLIFF
FOCUSED
PASSION
CREATIVE
DETERMINATE
ACHIEVE
CONCEPTUAL
DOING
ALPS
CARDIO
DETERMINATION
CHEERING
CONFIDENT
BEFORE
CAMERA
CHALLENGE
CROSS
ARMS
BOX
CONVICTION
CLIMBING
EXPRESSION
DETERMINED
SUCCESS
COMMITMENT
HEALTHY
METAPHOR
COUPLE
DEDICATION
GYM
HEAD
LIFTING
MUSCULAR
EXERCISE
TOGETHER
OUTDOORS
OBSTACLE
ORIENTATIONS
PEAK
PERSEVERANCE
TRAINING
OPEN
LEAVING
NOTEBOOK
IDEAS
NATURE
PASSIONATE
POWERFUL
RUNNING
WORKOUT
SEASIDE
HILL
TEAMWORK

1. **Determined people don't give up on their goal, regardless of how tough things get!**
   They understand how to harness their determination and will not give up. They have clear reasons why they must achieve their objective and what the consequences of failure are. The greater the consequences, the greater their level of determination.

2. **Determined people don't let failure stop them.**
   They understand that they may fail initially, and frequently, but they will eventually succeed. For them, failure builds resilience. They understand that the more they fail, the more resilient they will become, and they'll consequently become even more determined. They accept that it takes courage and self-belief to pick themselves back up after a failure, and it is their determination, with that resilience, that keeps them moving forward and trying again (and again).

3. **Determined people don't let the fear of failure stop them.**
   They know failure teaches you to value success. When they've been through periods of failure, and when success does come, they know not to take it for granted. They rightly feel that they

have really earned their success when they reflect back on the dark days when nothing was going right for them.

4. Determined people know that failure is a great teacher.

They understand that the experience and knowledge they gain when they encounter failure can be harnessed in the future to help them be successful in the long term. As long as they can identify why they failed, failure can be a brilliant teacher by helping them not make the same mistakes again.

5. Determined people don't let what they don't know stop them.

They're willing to ask lots of questions, and even 'fall on their face' a few times, until they achieve their goals. Study the lives of some of the world's greatest innovators, entrepreneurs, explorers, engineers, scientists, doctors and artists and you'll see that curiosity is one of the key ingredients that made them successful. People who are determined constantly ask questions.

6. Determined people don't fear rejection.

The greatest entrepreneurs, executives and salespeople are the ones who don't let rejection stop them. They know that the only way to overcome rejection is to keep going. Their reasons why they have to succeed are greater than their fear of not succeeding.

7. **Determined people are not impulsive.**
They are patient – willing to be prepared to wait until the right possibility or opportunity arises. They're willing to bide their time and accept that this may not be the right moment for them. But they know that one day a new possibility or opportunity will present itself to them, and they wait patiently for that day.

8. **Determined people are flexible and resourceful.**
Bashing your head against a brick wall, in the hope that it will break, is not determination. It's stupidity. Determined people will continue to try new things and keep changing their approach until they achieve their desired outcome. People who show determination are like a palm tree: they bend in the wind and always come back. The stubborn (who think they are determined, but actually are not) are often the ones who will end up broken and battered.

9. **Determined people work hard and work smart.**
They understand that they can't achieve any goal, big or small, without a strong work ethic. It's not just about effort itself, but also knowing what to focus their effort on. It's all about working hard but working smart as well.

One part of being inspired by someone else's achievements, like the trans-Atlantic rower Lee Spencer's, is that it can teach you the importance of determination in achieving meaningful success. It can inspire you to take on new, re-alistic, achievable opportunities. To help you do this you need to get into the habit of applying the nine behaviours listed above.

When you're determined to achieve something, and you actually achieve it, you'll find it will inspire you to take on even bigger, more meaningful and increasingly rewarding opportunities and objectives.

Even though being determined is a crucial element of achieving meaningful success, you won't achieve it without some help from other sources. This will come in the form of whom you chose to identify as your heroes, and which of your friends can best support you.

CHAPTER 11
THE HEROIC RWANDAN

IDENTIFYING YOUR HEROES

I want to introduce you to one of my heroes. He is Nicholas Hitimana, CEO of Ikirezi Natural Products, an agribusiness based in the central African nation of Rwanda. I have known Nicholas for many years, and I'm convinced his achievements as an entrepreneur surpass all of the great success stories from Silicon Valley.

You see, against all odds, Nicholas stuck to his belief in an idea that had the potential to bring huge, positive change into the lives of great numbers of people in Rwanda, who had been affected by the horrific genocide there. This belief, which he'd held since he was very young, was based on a simple principle. As he once told me, "I believe that people have in themselves the potential to get out of poverty if you create the right environment that allows them to do that."

That is his core belief and it has driven him to achieve real, sustainable entrepreneurial success and fundamentally change many people's lives for the better.

Nicholas was working for a World Bank agricultural project in Rwanda when the ethnic genocide began in April 1994. Over the course of 100 days, some 800,000 Rwandans were brutally murdered. Nicholas was able to escape with his wife and baby son, and ended up in Edinburgh in May 1995. He then pursued a master's programme in Rural Development at the University of Edinburgh, which he completed in 1996. Not being able to return to Rwanda immediately, he was encouraged by the university and his friends to pursue a PhD research programme, which he successful completed.

And here's what he did next.

In 2001, rather than getting a high-paying job in the West, Nicholas and his wife, Elsie, decided to return to Rwanda. They set out to look for new ways of creating meaningful employment, primarily for the widows and orphans of the genocide. With his agricultural specialization, and his vision, Nicholas was engaged by the Rwandan government to explore the possibility of producing essential oil from South African geranium seeds.

As a result, in 2006 Nicholas founded Ikirezi Natural Products, a community-interest company that produces high-quality essential oils to sell in both Rwanda and internationally. The profits from his company go to a series of cooperatives run by the workers to fund housing and educational projects.

Taken from an old Rwandan proverb, the word *ikirezi* means 'a precious pearl.' Nicholas views everyone who works at Ikirezi Natural Products as a unique person of innate value. Today, over 350 widows and poor farmers work for the operation.

But Ikirezi is not simply about employing people and giving them an income. It is about Nicholas's belief that the people who work there are 'precious pearls.' Whatever they've been through, he wants Ikirezi to create the right environment to allow them to heal and get out of poverty. More importantly, he wants it to give them back their self-respect and their confidence, so they can create a new and better future for themselves and for their families.

All of this is underpinned by his belief that people have in themselves the potential to get out of poverty if you create the right environment for them.

I have huge admiration for people who want to set up and run a business. However, it's one thing to start a company, grow it successfully and employ hundreds of people in places like the UK, Europe or the US. It takes someone with extraordinary entrepreneurial drive, talents and skills to start a business and make a success of it in a country where the idea of setting up any sort of venture would have been impossible not that long ago.

And that's why Nicholas is one of my heroes. His life, and what he stands for, has inspired me during difficult and challenging times. When I hear him talk, or chat with him on the phone, his advice motivates me to see new possibilities in both my private and professional life. His humility, wisdom, calmness, kindness and how he treats people should be the key attributes everyone aspires to.

And finally, on a personal level, Nicolas made me understand the importance of having your own heroes to help you on your path to meaningful success. Let's explore this further.

"AS YOU GET OLDER
IT IS HARDER TO
HAVE HEROES,
BUT IT IS SORT OF
NECESSARY."

Ernest Hemingway

THE IMPORTANCE
OF HEROES

A hero is someone who gives of themselves, often putting their own life at great risk, for the greater good. They're willing to make a personal sacrifice for the benefit of others. Crucially, research on heroes reveals a number of ways in which they inspire us, so that we can improve our lives.

Here are six benefits that heroes provide:

1. **Elevation.**
   Research from Jonathan Haidt, Professor of Ethical Leadership at New York University, suggests that heroes and heroic action may evoke a unique emotional response called 'elevation.' Haidt has done extensive research into its benefits.

   When people experience elevation, he found, they feel a mix of awe, reverence and admiration for a morally beautiful act. The emotion is described as being similar to calmness, warmth and love. Haidt says that elevation is "elicited by acts of virtue or moral beauty; it causes warm, open feelings in the chest."

2. **Storytelling.**
   Scott Allison, Professor of Psychology at the University of Richmond, in Virginia, highlights the

importance of storytelling. In ancient times, tribe members huddled around a communal fire at the end of each day for warmth and protection. But this activity had another crucial role: storytelling. Huddled together around the fire, stories of great heroic acts were shared.

These stories would have calmed people's fears, buoyed their spirits, nourished their hopes, and fostered important values of strength and resilience. Humans today are in many ways no different from our early ancestors. We're drawn to good hero stories because they comfort us and heal us, and that can provide greater purpose and meaning.

3. **Connections**.

Allison also sees storytelling as a community-building activity. For early humans, gathering around communal fires to hear stories helped establish social connections with others. This sense of family, group or community was, and remains, central to human emotional wellbeing.

Stories that feature heroes can also promote a strong sense of social identity. If the hero is an effective one, they perform actions that exemplify and affirm the group's most cherished values. The validation of a shared worldview, told vividly in storytelling, cements social bonds. Heroes are role models whose behaviours reinforce our most treasured values and connections with others.

4. Emotional Intelligence.

Bruno Bettelheim, a prominent Austrian psychoanalyst, believed that children's fairy tales are useful in helping people, especially youngsters, understand emotional experiences. The heroes of these tales are usually subjected to dark, foreboding experiences, such as encounters with witches, evil spells, abandonment, neglect, abuse and death. Hearing these tales can help children develop strategies for resolving their fears and distress.

Bettelheim believed that even the most distressing fairy tales, such as those by the Brothers Grimm, add clarity to confusing emotions and give people a greater sense of life's meaning and purpose. The darkness of fairy tales allows children to grow emotionally, developing their emotional intelligence and preparing them for the challenges of adulthood.

5. Transformation.

Joseph Campbell, Professor of Literature at Sarah Lawrence College in New York, studied similarities that ran through myths from different cultures. He identified shared themes and characteristics, and found that heroes undergo a personal transformation during their heroic journeys.

In every hero story, the hero starts out missing an important quality, usually self-confidence, humility, or a sense of his or her true purpose in life. To succeed, the hero must recover, or discover, this quality. Every hero story tells of a journey toward personal transformation. We can take inspiration from heroic tales to help us grow and find meaningful success.

6. **Generativity.**

The German-American psychologist Eric Erikson maintained that personality develops in a predetermined order, through eight stages of psychosocial development, from infancy to adulthood. He called stage 7 'generativity.'

Generativity refers to 'making your mark' on the world through creating or nurturing things that will outlast an individual. People who experience this need often have protégés or create positive changes that will benefit others. Heroic stories, Erikson suggests, inspire us to give back to the society that has given us so much.

Going back to Professor Haidt, the emotion of elevation provides us with the desire to become a better person. Elevation, he said, "motivates people to behave more virtuously themselves." The elevation we feel upon witnessing a heroic act inspires us to believe that we're capable of heroic acts ourselves.

YOUR
HERO

From all of this you can hopefully see the importance of identifying your heroes. People need heroes because heroes save or improve lives, and heroes are inspiring.

But we also need heroes for surprising reasons that go beyond the direct benefits of heroic action. Heroes elevate us emotionally – they help heal our psychological ills; build connections between people; encourage us to transform ourselves for the better; and call us to become heroes and help others.

Heroes take risks and do things that may cost them on a personal level. Their feats of derring-do may result in them being injured. They may have to forfeit something of value. They may even lose their life in pursuit of their heroic deed. But, despite it all, they're willing to take that risk – a risk on behalf of others.

Heroes may be just as afraid as the next person, and they may be just as aware of the danger they face. But they act *in spite of* their fear. They aren't some special class of human being who's exempt from the normal tendencies to be afraid in the face of danger. Knowing full well that danger lies ahead, they forge ahead just the same. Facing down your fears and courageously pressing on is heroic.

It is crucial, then, to identify your heroes, as they give you far more than inspiration. They will be your greatest teachers. Your heroes show you the secrets to unlocking your fullest potential as a human being.

To help you do this, I suggest you identify at least one hero in the four parts of your life. I am using the widest definitions here for these four parts:

- **Work.** It might be that you're conventionally employed, either full-time or part-time. Or, you might volunteer or be self-employed. Alternately, work could be an activity that you do in your spare time, like writing a book, painting or formulating a business idea.

- **Family.** This could be close family, distant cousins, aunties, uncles, nieces, nephews, your partner's family or relatives from the past.

- **Spiritual.** In general, spirituality is a sense of connection to something bigger than just yourself. If you don't believe in spirituality, then think of sporting, historical, political or cultural heroes.

- **Friends.** In Chapter 12, I'll examine the importance of friends and the eight vital support roles they fulfil. Try and identify those friends who've exhibited a heroic action that you really admire.

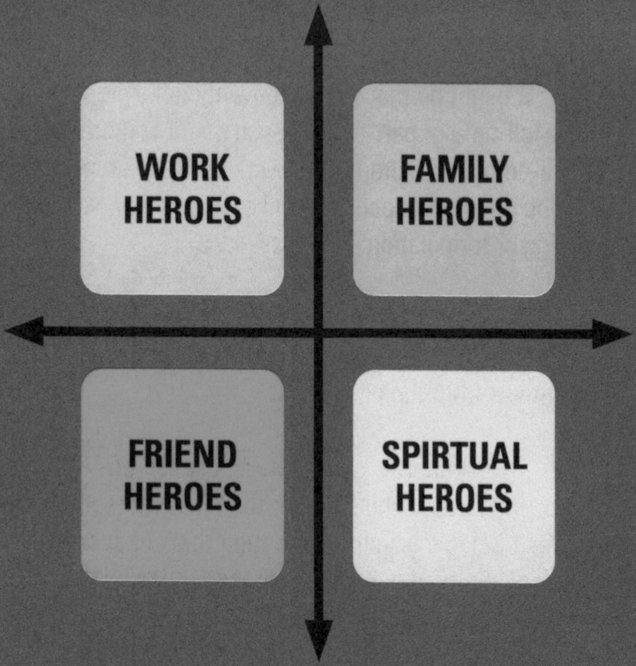
WORK HEROES
FAMILY HEROES
FRIEND HEROES
SPIRTUAL HEROES

Your heroes in each area must be people you find inspiring and motivating, because you admire one of their character traits, they've achieved what you are about to attempt, or you're in awe of what they do, or have done, in their lives.

These are the people who will help you achieve your plans, goals or dreams by showing ways to overcome obstacles, think in a different way or give you the motivation to keep going. They'll drive and push you along the path to success by providing inspiration from their lives when things get tough and challenging.

To find sources of inspiration to help you achieve meaningful success, just look at the lives of your heroes. You'll discover that your heroes will help you enormously in all aspects of your life.

CHAPTER 12
FRIENDS AND PARACHUTES
SEEKING TO COLLABORATE

July 2019 was the 50th anniversary of the first moon landing by astronauts Neil Armstrong, Buzz Aldrin and Mike Collins. There was wall-to-wall coverage on television, in newspapers, on the internet, in magazines and on the radio, recapping all aspects of that momentous event.

It's easy to fall into the trap of thinking, 50 years on, that the Apollo 11 mission could have been anything other than a success. From 1969-1972, NASA managed six moon landings, and even Apollo 13 – which had to abandon its landing after an explosion on board – returned its crew of three safely home.

However, everyone who worked at NASA during the 1960s and early 1970s knew all too well the risks.

There was no escaping the fact that the chances of failure were enormous.

Of the 967 NASA launches before Apollo 11, one in seven either failed to reach space, malfunctioned or blew up. The rocket that was to eventually transport Armstrong, Aldrin and Collins to the moon was the 111-metre Saturn V rocket. It carried 2.5 million kilograms of fuel which, if it combusted all at once, would have exploded with 4% of the energy of the bomb that destroyed Hiroshima.

With Saturn V weighing nearly 3 million kg, the astronauts knew the rocket would rise slowly at first but break the sound barrier in a minute. They had to work through numerous procedures and mathematical calculations to ensure that they could get to the moon's orbit at the right time, speed and angle of descent. The slightest misjudgement and they would miss the moon entirely... but they executed it all perfectly.

The astronauts landed on the moon with just 25 seconds of fuel left. To make navigation easier, they were dependent on the Eagle's landing module's onboard guidance computer. To put this into context, today, your mobile phone has more than a thousand times the processing power of the computer that landed man on the moon.

Leaving the moon required them to fire a separate part of the lunar module in which they'd touched down. The astronauts – with limited supplies of oxygen, food and fuel – rested their hopes on a single engine surviving the journey and the lunar landing. There was no 'Plan B' if it did not work.

So, why did NASA and the astronauts themselves still think that these significant risks, where failure could doom them at any moment, were worth taking? Although Apollo 11 relied on an extraordinary level of mathematics, engineering and software, rigorous testing and three incredibly brave men, there was something even more important at work.

On 25 May 1961, President John F Kennedy stood before Congress and proposed that the US "should commit itself to achieving the goal, before this decade is out, of landing a man on the Moon and returning him safely to the Earth." On 16 July 1969, Armstrong, Aldrin and Collins achieved that goal.

Armstrong summed up why they took all of these risks: "I believe that the message of Apollo 11 was that in the spirit of Apollo, a free and open spirit, you can attack a very difficult goal and achieve it, if you all agree and work together to achieve that goal."

The key piece in that equation is 'work together.' They took all these risks because everyone associated with the mission worked as a team. It was teamwork that inspired everyone to think and work together in their pursuit of a common goal.

The chances of you achieving your objectives and goals without a team supporting you are next to nothing. Whether you're planning to set up a business, train for a marathon, learn a new language, schedule a sabbatical, or pursue something else entirely, a strong, reliable team will prove invaluable.

This 'team' will probably include friends and family, but also some strangers. Let's first start with friends.

THE IMPORTANCE
OF FRIENDS

———

Tom Rath is an author and researcher who's spent the past two decades studying how work can improve human health and wellbeing. His ten books have sold more than ten million copies and are frequently on global bestseller lists.

Drawing on research and case studies from topics as diverse as management, marriage and architecture, Rath's book *Vital Friends* reveals what is common and essential for friendships: a regular focus on what each person is contributing to the friendship. He argues that mutual input into the friendship is necessary, rather than everything coming from one person who's expected to be everything.

The book builds on the idea that we all have strengths as people in general, but also as friends. This is evident from the different types of roles we take on as friends to each other. According to Rath, there are eight vital roles that close friends might play in any given situation. Some friends play only one role; a few play several; none play all of them unilaterally.

Here's a brief summary of Rath's eight roles that friends can offer:

- **Builder.** Builders are great motivators, always pushing you toward the finishing line. They continually invest in your development and genuinely want you to succeed.

- **Champion.** Champions stand up for you and what you believe in. They are loyal friends who sing your praises and will defend you until the end.

- **Companion.** A companion is always there for you, whatever the circumstances. You share a bond that is virtually unbreakable.

- **Connector.** Connectors are bridge-builders who help you to get what you want. They get to know you and then connect you to others.

- **Collaborator.** This is a friend with similar interests; someone you can easily relate to. You might share a passion for something such as sports, hobbies, religion, work, politics, food, music, films or books, for example.

- **Energizer.** These are your fun friends, who always give you a boost. You have more positive moments when you are with these friends.

- **Mind opener.** Mind openers are the friends who expand your horizons with new ideas, opportunities, cultures and people. They help you to create positive change.

- **Navigator.** These friends give you advice and keep you headed in the right direction. You go to them whenever you need guidance, and they talk through the pros and cons with you until you find an answer.

This might sound a bit clinical, but it's important to understand and accept that your friends provide you with different strengths in their support. These range from loyalty and shared interests to motivation, guidance, advice and counsel. The trick is to recognize that friends will give you different types of help and support along the road to achieving your objectives.

If you're inspired to take on a new challenge, write down from Rath's list of eight roles which friend will help you in a specific way. Use this friend's role tool to help you do this. Put a name next to the relevant role a friend could provide, to give you the help you need. You don't have to fill in all the roles.

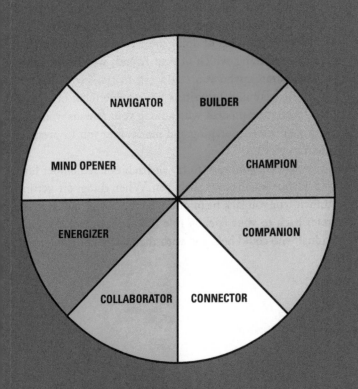

For example, if you were thinking of starting a business, which of your friends would be Connectors? Setting up and running a business is a difficult and challenging thing to do. Therefore, you'll likely have to expand your current network to include new people who could help you.

If you're thinking of doing a big bicycle ride, involving intensive training, which of your friends would you see as a Collaborator, who you could ask to train with you? If you were planning to write a book, which can be a long and frustrating process, who among your friends would be your Builder, encouraging and motivating you to press on and not give up?

Whatever you want to try and achieve, remember how much your friends could help you. When things are getting difficult, or you lack inspiration, or you've run out of ideas, refer back to your friends' role tool and contact the individual who could help you with that particular challenge.

"IN THE LONG HISTORY OF HUMANKIND (AND ANIMAL KIND, TOO) THAT THOSE WHO LEARNED TO COLLABORATE AND IMPROVISE MOST EFFECTIVELY HAVE PREVAILED."

Charles Darwin

WHO'S PACKING
YOUR PARACHUTE

———

Now, let's take a look at strangers, and how they can help you achieve extraordinary things.

Charlie Plumb was a US Navy jet pilot in Vietnam. After 75 combat missions, his plane was destroyed by a surface-to-air missile. Plumb ejected and parachuted into enemy hands. He was captured and spent six years in a communist North Vietnamese prison. He survived the ordeal and now lectures on the lessons he learned from that experience.

One day, when Plumb and his wife were sitting in a restaurant, a man at another table came up and said, "You're Plumb! You flew jet fighters in Vietnam from the aircraft carrier Kitty Hawk. You were shot down!"

"How in the world did you know that?" asked Plumb.

"I packed your parachute," the man replied.

The man shook his hand and said, "I guess it worked!" Plumb assured him, "It sure did. If your chute hadn't worked, I wouldn't be here today."

Plumb couldn't sleep that night, thinking about that man. "I kept wondering what he might have looked like in a Navy uniform: a white hat, a bib in the back and bell-bottom trousers," he said. "I wonder how many times I might have seen him and not even said, 'Good morning, how are you?' Or anything, because, you see, I was a fighter pilot, and he was just a sailor."

Plumb thought of the man-hours the sailor had spent at a long wooden table in the bowels of the ship, carefully weaving the shrouds and folding the silks of each chute, holding in his hands each time the fate of someone he didn't know.

Plumb says that everyone has someone who provides what they need to make it through the day.

So, who's packing your parachute? How many strangers provide you with 'the tools' to achieve your goals? Or, to simply make it through the day?

Going back to that big bike ride you're training for, think of how many people and hours were dedicated to designing and producing the helmet that could save your life if you crash. Or that book you're writing – think about all those engineers and designers who produced the software that allows you to write it quickly and securely, automatically corrects spelling mistakes, suggests better words, and allows you to save various versions and send it to your publisher. Or that business idea you have, that was sparked by an article you'd read in a newspaper. Think of the journalist who wrote it, the research they had to do and the deadline they were under to get it published and into your hands.

In your life, in both the personal and work-related things you want to achieve, many people have packed your parachute. Without you even being aware of these people, they've probably been sources of inspiration.

Recognizing that, and being grateful, will help you to understand and appreciate that many strangers will be supporting you in achieving your goals and objectives.

There will be many people in your virtual team – friends, acquaintances and complete strangers – and fully acknowledging how important they are will be integral to you being successful. Knowing that you aren't alone, in whatever you want to achieve, should provide you with confidence and inspiration

With a defined purpose, a mindset of a younger version of you, a proactive and determined attitude, and supported by your heroes, friends and sources of inspiration, you can now choose the goals that will help you to finally achieve meaningful and rewarding success.

CHAPTER 13
FORMULAS AND TRICKS

SETTING THE RIGHT GOALS

While writing this book, I witnessed what was one of the most remarkable and inspiring comebacks in the world of sports – Tiger Woods winning the Masters Tournament.

The win surprised everyone, not only in the world of golf, but sports fans in general. Popular opinion was that Woods was a spent force and, at age 44, the chances of him winning a championship again were slim. But to put winning the 2019 Masters in context, you need to look back over the previous 25 years of his golfing career.

In 1997, at just 21, Woods had his first major win, at the Masters. Over the next 11 years, he won another 13 majors. In the noughties, he spent the most consecutive weeks (281) being the number one golfer in world – a record that has not been beaten since. However, the next decade of Woods' career was marked both by personal problems and injuries, and most golf experts believed that there was little chance of him winning any golf competition again.

So, winning the 2019 Masters was an extraordinary achievement. Jack Nicklaus, arguably the most successful golfer of all time, tweeted: "A big 'well done' from me to @ TigerWoods! I am so happy for him and for the game of golf. This is just fantastic!!!" Serena Williams tweeted: "I am literally in tears watching @TigerWoods. This is Greatness like no other. Knowing all you have been through physically to come back and do what you did today. Wow. Congrats a million times! I am so inspired thank you buddy." And Barack Obama tweeted: "Congratulations, Tiger. To come back and win the Masters after all the highs and lows is a testament to excellence, grit and determination."

But why does this particular win inspire such reactions? It's more than a comment on Woods' golf game and athletic brilliance. Witnessing someone at their very best is, in its own way, inspiring. But what is even more inspiring is that as a child he set a personal goal of beating Nicklaus' record of winning 20 Majors. And he's still driven to achieve it.

This was a win for having goals, and for going through bad times and coming out the other side.

Just stop for a minute and think of something you really wanted 20 years ago, or a project you started in 1997. Well, are you still trying to achieve it? Are you still driven to reach that goal? Do you think about it every day? Woods' frailties have made him more relatable in recent years, but it's always been his superhuman determination that inspires awe. In the 1980s he set out a goal and today he's still working to achieve it.

In Woods' 2019 Masters win press conference, he said this: "People have struggles in their lives, personal struggles, physical struggles, and you've overcome these things." A reporter then asked him, "What message might you say to people who are struggling?" Woods thought for a moment. "Well, you never give up," he said. "That's a given. You always fight. Giving up's never in the equation."

Here are some ideas to help you not give up on your goals. As you will see, setting the right type of goals, and having strategies so that you don't give up, are critical for meaningful success.

IS THERE A MAGIC FORMULA TO GOAL SETTING?

As it turns out, there is a tried-and-true formula. A study from the Dominican University of California looked at both goal setting and actual strategies for achieving goals.

Dr Gail Matthews of the school's Psychology Department recruited 267 participants from businesses, organizations and networking groups throughout the US and overseas for a look at how to achieve goals. Participants ranged in age from 23–72 and came from a wide variety of backgrounds and occupations.

Matthews found that more than 70% of the participants – who recorded their progress, and sent weekly updates to a friend – reported that they'd accomplished their goal or were nearly there. On the other hand, 30% of the group – a segment that did not write their goals down, and kept them entirely to themselves – made significantly less progress.

What the findings showcased was that the participants who reaped the best results followed a specific model:

- **Commit to Action.**
  Rather than simply writing down a goal, the group was asked to commit to an action. Essentially, they were making a commitment on paper to achieve their goal.

- **Accountability to Peers.**
  This group had to follow up on their concrete goal planning and action commitment by enlisting another person. They needed to send their commitment to a peer, making them more accountable.

- **Regular Updates.**
  This group had to update their friend or accountability person on a weekly basis, which kept them focused on their progress.

Matthews became interested in studying procrastination after reading an article in *Fast Company* magazine about "The 1953 Yale Study of Goals." The premise of the study – that people who write down specific goals for their future are far more likely to be successful than those who have either unwritten goals or no specific goals at all – has inspired the teachings of many self-help authors and personal coaches.

The only trouble is that the study was never actually conducted! The 1996 *Fast Company* article debunked the Yale study as little more than an often-quoted urban legend.

However, Matthews' research now backs up the conclusions long attributed to the mythical Yale study. "With the proliferation of business and personal coaching, and the often anecdotal reports of coaching success, it is important that this growing profession be founded on sound scientific research," Matthews said. "My study provides empirical evidence for the effectiveness of three coaching tools: accountability, commitment, and writing down one's goals."

TRICKING YOUR BRAIN INTO ACHIEVING GOALS

In a fascinating article for the *Psychology Today* website, "The Science of Accomplishing Your Goals," Dr Ralph Ryback, a psychiatrist affiliated with Boston City Hospital and Harvard Medical School, suggests three ways to trick your brain into helping you accomplish your goals.

1. **Turn goals into habits.**

   First, turn the pursuit of your goal into a regular habit. Dr Ryback cites a recent study published in the scientific journal *Neuron* that found that habits and goals are stored differently in the human brain. To help you form positive habits, you need to be consistent. Work toward your goal every day, even if you don't feel like it. Either set aside a specific time each day, or a specific context, to actively pursue it. For instance, if you want to start running every day, try and do it at the same time every day (a specific *time*), or do it just before you have breakfast (a specific *context*). The more regular the behaviour, the more easily your brain can convert it into a habit.

2. Change your environment.

Sometimes, all you need is a different setting. Environmental cues are essential when it comes to habit formation, in part because the brain is excellent at connecting an environment with a specific situation. If you find yourself constantly giving up on your goals, then take a look at your surroundings. When you visit your favourite coffee shop, do you seem to zone out as you try to get down to work? If so, try a different coffee shop or work in your local library.

According to journalist Charles Duhigg, author of *The Power of Habit*, the best time to change a habit is on holiday because your usual environmental cues are missing. So, next time you fly off to somewhere special, take the opportunity to reassess what goals you really want to achieve.

3. Use your dopamine loads.

When we get something we want, such as a promotion, a lovely meal or a catch-up with a good friend, our brain releases dopamine. This chemical is often called the 'feel good' neurotransmitter because it does just that – it makes us feel good.

It's possible to manipulate your dopamine levels by setting small goals and then accomplishing them. This is one reason people benefit from to-do lists;

the satisfaction that comes with ticking off a small task brings a flood of dopamine. Each time your brain gets a whiff of this chemical messenger, it will want you to repeat the associated behaviour.

The next time you set out to accomplish a big goal, try breaking it down into bite-sized, dopamine-friendly pieces.

For instance, if you want to go to the gym every day, check off each successful workout on a calendar. If you want to write a novel, make a deal with yourself to write for just 15 minutes every day, and make note of your completed writing sessions on a wall chart.

Stay consistent, change your environment, bask in the dopamine, and you'll be able to trick your brain into helping you achieve your goals.

A PERSONAL
EXAMPLE

In 2013, I published my first book, *Changing Course*, which was inspired by the stroke I suffered in 2006, at the age of 41. In the book, I discuss finding your personal vision and your overall goals in life.

Here are some of those reflections:

"Imagine it's ten years on from today, and you've been invited to a party to celebrate a decade of your new life. The key people in your world are there – your family and your friends. Each of them has been asked to speak about you for five minutes, outlining what you've achieved over the past ten years.

"How would you want them to describe your life, your character, your mindset, since you changed course?

"Your answer to this will be your personal vision, your overall goal, your quest.

"When I do this exercise, I imagine what one of my closest friends will say about me. It's a great motivator when I have writer's block, or when I'm tempted to do things which, on paper, might earn me more money, but give me little personal satisfaction:

"Over the last ten years Neil has written four books which have had a positive impact on people's lives."

Seven years later, here I am, writing this, my fourth book. I hope this demonstrates the importance of goal setting.

Looking back to when I set myself the goal of writing *Changing Course*, I inadvertently adopted the advice on goal-setting from both Dr Gail Matthews and Dr Ralph Ryback.

I had to commit to action because I'd told family and friends of my goal, which made me accountable. I kept them regularly updated on my progress. I got into the habit of writing at the same time each day, although I would switch-up environments. Finally, I had a wall planner in my office that broke down the book into specific chapters, indicating when a certain chapter had to be completed. When I'd finished that chapter, I would tick it off on the wall planner.

I've used the same goal strategy for writing all four of my books.

But, before you pat yourself on your back, believing that all future possibilities, opportunities and success with the goals you achieve will be strictly attributable to your hard work and effort, it may be time to rethink that.

CHAPTER 14

RANDOM EVENTS

ACCEPTING LUCK

On 26 November 1983, in Hickory, California, an industrial paper salesman and a mathematics teacher had a son, Chris. Seven months later, on 14 May 1984, in White Palins, New York, a dentist and a psychiatrist had a son called Mark. Eight days after that, on 22 May, in Gainesville, Florida, a psychiatrist and a teacher had a son they named Dustin.

Eighteen years on, Chris, Mark and Dustin were about to start their second year at Harvard University.

Tucked away in an office on the Harvard campus, an accommodation officer ran a computer programme that assigned students to their rooms for the year ahead. A printer jumped to life, producing the lists of who would reside where.

The lists were then pinned to notice boards in the school's various dormitories and houses.

The next day, when second-year students arrived on campus, Chris, Mark and Dustin learned that they'd be living together in Room H33 of a red brick residence called Kirkland House.

These three young men were Chris Hughes, Mark Zuckerberg and Dustin Moskovitz, who later, from Room H33, founded Facebook.

That computer programme that randomly put the three together helped start one of the biggest companies in the world. In that room, the 'chemistry' between Hughes, Moskovitz and Zuckerberg fuelled a creative flow of ideas around building a social networking platform.

Because they were thrown together in that student residence, Hughes, Moskovitz and Zuckerberg are now millionaires or billionaires. They've changed the way we all communicate, self-identify and share details of our lives. In doing so, they've inspired so many other entrepreneurs. It would be easy to conclude that at the core of their success lay their creativity, talents, skills and hard work.

But is that the whole picture? Was something else – something more fundamental – part of the mix? Well, Hughes hints at what this could be in his book, *Fair Shot: Rethinking Inequality and How We Earn*.

"Saying people get lucky is not a denial that they work hard and deserve positive outcomes," he wrote. "It is a way of acknowledging that in a winner-take-all economy, small, chance encounters – like who you sit down next to at a dinner party or who your college roommate is – have a more significant impact than they have ever had before. In some cases, the collections of these small differences can add up to create immense fortunes."

Just think about what Hughes was saying. As improbable as it sounds, what seem like small, random events, like chance encounters, can end up having the most significant impact on your life.

So, here's a question: how successful do you think you've been so far in your life? And by success I don't just mean how much money you've earned or how senior a role you have in an organization. Consider other indicators of success: what professional qualifications you've achieved; whether you're currently employed and secure in that job; if you're raising a family; if you have free time to do things you enjoy doing; if you're at ease and generally happy.

Hopefully, most of us would say that we *have* been successful in these important aspects of our lives.

Then, ask yourself this: how much of the success you've achieved so far can you attribute to your own actions – to your effort, work and input? And, how much is down to chance, to factors beyond your control, like who you sit next to at a dinner, meet on a plane or room with in college?

Personally, I would attribute 55% to my own effort and achievement and 45% to factors beyond my control.

But let's think about this. In the end, is it not 100% due to factors beyond my control? Just think about Hughes, Moskovitz and Zuckerberg – if that computer programme hadn't placed these three together in room H33, Facebook might never have been founded and my bet is that they wouldn't be as wealthy and successful as they are now.

Warren Buffet, the investor and philanthropist, calls this the ovarian lottery:

"The truth is, I'm here in my position as a matter of luck. When I was born in 1930, odds were probably 40 to 1 against me being born in the United States. I did win the ovarian lottery on that first day, and on top of that, I was male. Put that down as another 50/50 shot and now the odds are 80 to 1 against being born a male in the United States, and it was enormously important in my whole life. To think that that makes me superior to anyone else as a human being is just... I can't follow that line of reasoning."

Setting the stage for Buffet's extraordinary success is the fact that he was born in the US as a white man. Basically, he was incredibly lucky, and he recognizes how these factors allowed him to achieve success with more ease than someone with a different demographic profile.

"I WANDERED
EVERYWHERE,
THROUGH CITIES AND
COUNTRIES WIDE.
AND EVERYWHERE
I WENT, THE WORLD
WAS ON MY SIDE."

Roman Payne

THE OVARIAN
LOTTERY

———

Let's look at it from a different point of view, using me as an example of someone who's benefitted from the ovarian lottery.

None of the following were my choice: I was born in England, one of the wealthiest countries in the world. I went to a primary school where I was taught to read. Today there are about 760 million adults in the world who are illiterate – that's more than the population of Europe, or 1 in ever 10 people alive on Earth today. Because I could read, I was able to get a good education from a variety of schools. Some 264 million children never get a chance to go to school. Because I got a good education, I was able to take exams and go to college. In the developing world, less than 3% of the population has an opportunity to pursue higher education.

I could go on about all of my jobs, the person I married and the children we had. But, hopefully, you get my point. Like Buffet, I'm incredibly lucky. Lucky to be born in the 20th century, and immensely lucky that my annual income allows me to be in the top 1% of earners in the world. If you have an annual income of £25,000 (about $31,500 US) or above, you're also in that enviable bracket.

Like Buffet, many of the things I've achieved so far in my life are down to sheer luck.

So, given all that, what proportion of the success you've achieved can you ascribe to your own achievement? Well, if you strip it all back, the logical answer is 0%. I hate to burst your bubble if you feel your successes have been achieved purely by hard work and determination. These are the by-products of the fact that your successes are fundamentally based on things over which you have no control whatsoever.

In the final analysis, you haven't really earned your achievements.

THE PRIDE
ILLUSION

The more you start to understand and accept that any success in your life has been largely attributable to luck, you realize that the shackles of your perceived success have not solely been down to your hard work and effort. The consequences of any further success will still be due to luck. Who knows who you will meet over the next week, month – or in the coming years – who will change the direction of your life in ways you can't even envisage today?

However, there is a significant caveat to all of this. Whatever future success you achieve, by all means strive to be humble. The greater your success, the humbler you should become.

Today, within a few seconds, you can post on Facebook, LinkedIn, Instagram or Twitter about another success in your life, for all your followers to see. Instead, hold back, do not press send and think what you're about to do. Those who do pat themselves on the back – and I've been guilty of this behaviour many times – have been taken in by the 'pride illusion.' Using social media to share inspiring stories, practical and helpful information or causes you feel passionately about is great, but don't bang your own drum. It's better to let others do that, if and when they really want to.

So, what should you do? It's simple: be grateful.

Gratitude has positive health implications. It's been shown to strengthen the immune system, lower blood pressure and enable better sleep. It can help reduce anxiety and depression. It strengthens the belief that life is meaningful and manageable. Gratitude has a powerful and lasting effect in that it can help reframe experiences in a positive way.

Gratitude is associated with how satisfied you are in life. The greater your gratitude, the happier you'll feel. All of this is well documented by respected scientists and medical experts.

People who have a grateful nature are more likely to be happy. In a TED Talk entitled, "Want to be happy? Be grateful," the Benedictine monk David Steindl-Rast explains that happiness does not make us grateful, but it is gratefulness that makes us happy. There are people who seem to have everything, he said – money, a huge house, a holiday home, a flashy wardrobe and expensive cars – but they can still be unhappy because they constantly want more. Conversely, there are those who've had big setbacks and difficult experiences in their lives, but they seem quite contented. That is, in part, because they are grateful.

When given a real gift, Steindl-Rast suggests – a gift that you haven't bought, earned or worked for, but that you see as valuable – the natural response is to show gratitude.

The biggest gift you've been given is that you were probably a winner of the ovarian lottery. Yes, when luck provides you with a new possibility or opportunity, you'll have to work hard and dedicate a lot of time and effort to achieving meaningful success. But never forget the random event that set you on this path to success – you were lucky and should therefore be grateful.

In the last 14 chapters I have tried to provide you with a path that will inspire you to achieve meaningful success. I've laid a foundation from which you can find inspiration, exposed the things that could block the path to inspiration, and explored ideas and experiences that can lead you to find your sources of inspiration.

All of this, if taken seriously and truly woven into your life, will lead you to discover that meaningful and rewarding success is about living your life in such a way that your legacy will inspire others to find their own meaningful success.

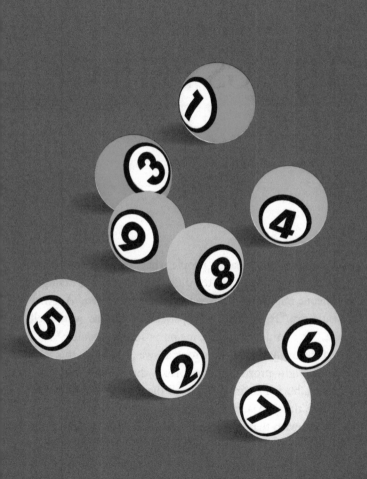

CHAPTER 15
LEAVING THINGS BEHIND
THE RIGHT LEGACY

If you asked ten separate people what the purpose of their life is, you'd probably get ten different answers. For example, someone might reply, "To be happy and contented." Another would say, "To explore and experience." Another would tell you, "To do things that give me purpose and meaning."

Obviously, there is no wrong answer, but I love this wise and thought-provoking quote from the novelist and journalist Chuck Palahniuk: "We all die. The goal isn't to live forever, the goal is to create something that will."

And with that in mind, I recently read an article about the self-made millionaire and philanthropist Eugene Lang.

In 1981, Lang looked out at the faces of the 61 sixth graders who had come to hear him speak. Years earlier,

Lang had attended this same school in East Harlem. Now, he wondered how he could get them to listen to him. What could he say to inspire these 11-year-olds from the rough and tumble streets of Upper Manhattan?

He had intended to say, "Work hard and you'll succeed," but on the way to the podium, the principal told him that three-quarters of the students would probably never finish high school.

And so, Lang made an impromptu change in direction and promised college tuition to every sixth grader who stuck it out through high school and graduated. Lang told the class about witnessing Dr Martin Luther King, Jr's famous "I Have a Dream" speech at the 1963 March in Washington. He urged the youngsters to dream their own dreams, and promised to do all he could to help them achieve their goals.

At that moment, he changed the life of every student in that room. For the first time, they had hope – hope of achieving more than their older brothers and sisters, hope of living a better life than their parents and neighbours.

A few years later, in 1986, Lang founded the I Have a Dream Foundation, which works to give all children the opportunity to pursue higher education, live up to their potential and achieve their dreams. It empowers children and students ('Dreamers') in under-resourced communities to graduate from college by equipping them with the skills and knowledge to succeed in postsecondary school, along with tuition support to remove financial barriers.

Today, 18,000 Dreamers have been through the programme in 28 states, and it has been rolled out internationally.

I don't know why or by whom Lang was invited to speak at his former school, but the outcome has been that thousands of disadvantaged students were given the opportunity to better their lives by getting an education.

As American philosopher William James once said, "The great use of life is to spend it for something that will outlast it." Lang could have spent his life concentrating solely on self-centred activities, and keeping his enormous fortune for himself and those close to him. But he did not. He realized back in 1981 that because of his wealth he had the opportunity to affect the lives of the disadvantaged students who live in East Harlem.

By the time he died in 2017, Lang's I Have a Dream Foundation had supported well over 18,000 students. But he also left something else. His story and his legacy will inspire so many in showing the importance of supporting the disadvantaged and the marginalized. During his lifetime he donated over $150 million to charities and institutions.

His legacy, among many other things, is that he spent most of his life doing things that outlasted him. And to me, that is a perfect legacy.

LEAVING
A LEGACY

———

What do we mean when we talk about leaving a legacy? My guess is that for a lot of people it means leaving money to someone or something they care about. It might be making a large bequest to the university you went to, or to a charity that was important in your life, or passing on a significant estate to your family. But surely, the definition is broader than that.

In her book, *The Well-Lived Life: Live with Purpose and Be Remembered*, Canadian sociologist and researcher Lyndsay Green suggests that leaving a legacy is not necessarily just about money.

"We are all leaving a legacy, whether we like it or not," said Green. "Our legacy is a combination of the way we live every day and the impact it has on our friends, our family, our community and the world, as well as how we prepare others for life without us. Leaving a legacy is a way to let others appreciate our love and our consideration for them, because we took the time to plan ahead for the impact our absence would have on them."

You don't have to become a tech mogul, premier footballer or a movie star earning millions to live a life of significance. All you have to do is share some parts of your life with others. However insignificant you may think they are, your experience, talent, time and ideas are often of greater value to others than you realise. That is your legacy.

"THE GREAT
USE OF LIFE IS
TO SPEND IT
FOR SOMETHING
THAT WILL
OUTLAST IT."

William James

SHARE YOUR
EXPERIENCE

Everybody has a story to tell – the story about the important achievements they've had in their life. They could be such accomplishments as bringing up a family, working for the same company for 30 years, pulling off a sporting feat, starting a business, dedicating time to a charity or looking after an older relative.

Whatever it is, your life is surely packed with experience. It's rich with lessons you've learned from life. So, share your life experiences. One way others could benefit might be that, based on your example and learning, they don't end up making the same mistakes you did. On the upside, they could embrace and try to replicate the experiences that led you to success, whatever that turned out to be.

Share those experiences with people you know who stand to benefit from them.

Share your experience.
Everybody has a story to tell – the story about the important achievements they've had in their life. They could be such accomplishments as bringing up a family, working for the same company for 30 years, pulling off a sporting feat, starting a business, dedicating time to a charity or looking after an older relative.

Whatever it is, your life is surely packed with experience. It's rich with lessons you've learned from life. So, share your life experiences. One way others could benefit might be that, based on your example and learning, they don't end up making the same mistakes you did. On the upside, they could embrace and try to replicate the experiences that led you to success, whatever that turned out to be.

Share those experiences with people you know who stand to benefit from them.

Share your talent.
There's something especially rewarding about applying your talents for the benefit of others. By recognizing and making the most of your talents, you contribute greatly to working with and helping others. Applying your talents to something bigger than yourself – a team's goal, a charity, a professional association or a community project – increases the chances of that endeavour being a success.

Share your time.
It's a paradox of life that only by giving away our time do we make our lives meaningful, and in turn help others find meaning. You can't put a monetary value on the time we spend kicking back with a family member, chatting with

a friend who is ill, supporting and mentoring a colleague, or helping those in need in our community... but it's so valuable for others.

Share your important ideas.
Sharing your ideas and insights in a letter or an email to those you love and admire is a brilliant thing to do. That could be someone who's been influential in your life, or relatives with whom you want to share your family history and core values. It could be someone you want to inspire with something that turned out to be important in your life. Or, it could be someone who played a major role in your life, who you'd like to thank. Whoever it is, sharing these things will inspire and motivate others.

Putting some of these suggestions into action will hopefully create an inspiring legacy, for you and for those in the future who may be inspired by your life and times. More crucially, they will give you meaning and purpose in themselves. Your life will be far more fulfilling – just take a look at Eugene Lang's life and legacy.

Leaving a legacy really is a win-win for every-one involved.

INSPIRED
THINKING

———

I started this book with a sad, but ultimately inspirational, story – the story of Becca Henderson. Her legacy inspired me to write it in the first place. And, in turn, I hope this book will provide many of you with various sources of inspiration that will lead to meaningful success.

Throughout these 15 chapters I have tried to share sources of inspiration through stories, ideas and strategies around the importance of themes like personal value, individuality, risk, blind self, self-belief, triviality, heroes, determination, goals, collaboration, passion, proactivity, staying young, being lucky, and legacy.

When you discover the feeling of inspiration in new things you do, there is a surge of energy, with a thrilling feeling of elevation and excitement. Your senses are amplified, and you're far more aware of the possibilities that seem to be opening up for you. It feels like you've been provided with a new perception, a new way to see things. All of this will lead you to find meaning and purpose in your life.

I hope, in reading this, that you feel inspired to do something new or different that engages you in ways that you haven't been engaged before. I hope that you feel driven and energized to do things, and change things, that will enhance your life and lead you to meaningful success.

As Pablo Picasso said, "Inspiration exists, but it has to find you working."

Inspired thinking is not a prescriptive thing – you cannot force yourself to be inspired. What you can do is seek out sources of inspiration, and that may take time and effort. But, ultimately, if you can open yourself up to new possibilities and opportunities, you will find life more rewarding and meaningful.

And, surely, that is the real definition of success.

> "ALL WE HAVE TO DECIDE IS WHAT TO DO WITH THE TIME THAT IS GIVEN TO US."

JRR Tolkien

REFERENCES
AND RESOURCES

OPENING QUOTE

Coelho, Paulo. *The Alchemist*. New York: HarperCollins, 1995.

INTRODUCTION

"Rebecca Henderson: Posthumous degree for rucksack heart woman."
  BBC News. 24 May 2019. https://bbc.in/2uwusuy.

Sivers, Derek. "You Need More Than Just Inspiration To Spark Brilliant
  Ideas." *Business Insider*. 15 April 2013. https://bit.ly/2tGbqSE.

Schwantes, Marcel. "15 Kobe Bryant Quotes From His Legendary Career
  That Will Inspire You." *Inc*. 26 January 2020. https://www.inc.com/
  marcel-schwantes/15-kobe-bryant-quotes-from-his-legendary-career-
  that-will-inspire-you.html.

Kaufman, Scott Barry. "Why Inspiration Matters." *Harvard Business Review*.
  8 November 2011. https://bit.ly/2sVizxN.

Thrash, Todd; and Elliot, Andrew F. "Inspiration as a psychological
  construct." *Journal of Personality and Social Psychology*. April 2003.
  https://bit.ly/2TY1rma.

CHAPTER 1   WHAT ARE THE ODDS

Brown, Deborah; Quinn, Kelly; and Brierley, Jenny. Buckton Vale Primary
  School. "Got kids heading for SATs? Read this!" *This Morning* ITV. 11
  May 2015. https://bit.ly/3aAMvjM.

Robbins, Mel. "How to stop screwing yourself over." *TED Talk*. June 2011.
  https://bit.ly/37vx22A.

Binazi, Ali. "Are You a Miracle?" *Huffington Post*. 16 June 2011.
  https://bit.ly/2tPjKzm.

Clark, Andrew; and Chalmers, David. "The extended mind." 23 October 1998.
  http://consc.net/papers/extended.html.

Ramachandran, VS. *The Tell-Tale Brain*. London: Windmill Books, 2012.

Yampolsky, Sofya. "What Are The Odds?" Visually. 10 November 2019.
https://bit.ly/35nAPyR.

CHAPTER 2   THINK DIFFERENT

Siltanen, Rob. "The Real Story Behind Apple's 'Think Different' Campaign."
Forbes. 14 December 2011. https://bit.ly/37xPeJ6.

Zimbardo, Phillip. "Stanford Prison Experiments." *Social Psychology Network*.
1971. https://bit.ly/3aGRvn9.

Fredrickson, Barbara Lee. "The Role of Positive Emotions in Positive
Psychology." *American Psychology*. 24 June 2011. https://www.ncbi.nlm.
nih.gov/pmc/articles/PMC3122271/.

CHAPTER 3   THE MINORITY

Seales, Rebecca. "This little-known inventor has probably saved your life."
BBC News. 18 July 2019. https://bbc.in/30RV2dK.

"Melinda Gates: Biography." IMDb. https://imdb.to/2xsM0tn.

Dunbar, Kevin; and Dumas, Denis. "The Creative Stereotype Effect."
PLoS One. 10 February 2016. https://bit.ly/2RRUQa6.

CHAPTER 4   INVISIBLE BARRIERS

Judkins, Rod. *Change your Mind*. Richmond, Australia: Hardie Grant, 2013.

Luft, Joseph; and Ingham, Harrington. "The Johari Window: a graphic
model of interpersonal awareness." *Proceedings of the Western Training
Laboratory in Group Development, University of California,
Los Angeles*. 1955.

Handy, Charles. *21 Ideas for Managers*. San Francisco: Jossey-Bass, 2000.

Malandro, Loretta. *Fearless Leadership*. New York: McGraw-Hill
Education, 2009.

Picoult, Jodi. *Vanishing Acts*. Hodder Paperbacks, 2014.

CHAPTER 5   FAKING IT

Gross, Terry. "Tom Hanks Says Self-Doubt Is 'A High-Wire Act That We
All Walk.'" *National Public Radio*. 26 April 2016. https://n.pr/2GpzHPs

Miller, Julie. "Why Emma Watson Sometimes Feels Like An 'Imposter'
in Hollywood." *Vanity Fair*. 3 August 2015. https://bit.ly/2HTZIY1.

Sakulku, Jaruwan; and Alexander, James. "The Imposter Phenomenon." *International Journal of Behavioral Science*. Vol. 6, No. 1: 75–97. 2011. https://bit.ly/2RNZaYd.

Young, Valerie. *The Secret Thoughts of Successful Women: Why Capable People Suffer from Impostor Syndrome and How to Thrive in Spite of It*. Random House 2011.

Young, Valerie. "The 5 Types of Imposters." Imposter Syndrome. 2019. https://bit.ly/310Yl2j.

CHAPTER 6   THE FOCUSING ILLUSION

Schwantes, Marcel. "Warren Buffett says this is what he'd do to live a happier life." *CNBC*. 8 November 2019. https://bit.ly/2Gruwyv.

Kahneman, Daniel. "2011: What scientific concept would improve everybody's cognitive toolkit?" *Edge*. https://www.edge.org/response-detail/11984.

Kahneman, Daniel; Kruger, Alan; Schkade, David; Schwarz, Norbert; and Stone, Arthur. "Would You Be Happier If You Were Richer? A Focusing Illusion." Princeton University Center for Economic Policy Studies. 7 May 2006. https://bit.ly/2RvP2EA.

Dobelli, Rolf. *The Art of The Good Life*. London: Sceptre, November 2017.

Xu, Jing; and Schwartz, Norbert. "How do you feel while driving your car? Depends on how you think about it." Ross School of Business, University of Michigan. 23 June 2006. https://bit.ly/3aMtuLq.

PART 3   IDEAS THAT LEAD TO THE SOURCES OF INSPIRATION

Frost, Robert. *The Road Not Taken and Other Poems*. New York: Penguin Random House, 2015 Anniversary Edition.

CHAPTER 7   BRILLIANT HANNAH

"Homepage." *Communitea*. 2019. www.communitea.me.

Khazan, Olga. "'Find Your Passion' Is Awful Advice." *The Atlantic*. 12 July 2018. https://bit.ly/36sCjXd.

O'Keefe, Paul; Dweck, Carol; and Walton, Gregory. "Implicit Theories of Interest: Finding Your Passion or Developing It?" *Association for Psychological Science*. 6 September 2018. https://bit.ly/30YLa23.

Michelle George; Ikigai Model Graphic.

CHAPTER 8   SPIRIT OF ADVENTURE

Purves, Libby. "Our spirit of adventure lives for ever." *The Times*. 6 May 2019. https://bit.ly/2O4VmAF.

Rippon, Isla; and Steptoe, Andrew. "Feeling Old vs Being Old; Associations Between Self-Perceived Age and Mortality." *Journal of the American Medical Association*. February 2015. https://bit.ly/2RWlQWf.

Lindner, Nicholas M; and Nosek, Brian A. "Dimensions of Subjective Age Identity Across the Lifespan." University of Virginia. Project Implicit. 6 June 2018. https://bit.ly/2uFcUfG.

Hanson, Sarah; and Jones, Andy. "USA Research shows group walking cuts risk of life-threating conditions." *Science Daily*. 19 January 2015. https://bit.ly/38JFuvq.

Sheppard, Cassandra. "The Neuroscience of Singing." *Uplift*. 11 December 2016. https://bit.ly/2Icou5C.

Tessman, Renee. "Speaking a Second Language May Delay Different Dementias." *American Academy of Neurology*. 6 November 2013. https://bit.ly/2whw1xw.

CHAPTER 9   RUNNING NICK

Covey, Stephen. *The 7 Habits of Highly Effective People*. New York: Simon and Schuster, 1999.

Burgess, Kaya. "Nick Butter: Around the World in 196 Marathons (That's One in Every Country)." *The Times*. 11 November 2019. https://bit.ly/2GufqYU.

Hansen, Drew. "Why Richard Branson And I Always Carry A Notepad." *Forbes*. 15 August 2011. https://bit.ly/30XOaLS.

"Walt Disney: Biography." *Biography*.Last updated 21 August 2019. https://bit.ly/3ck9TDf.

Berger, Sally. "The Secret of Getting Ahead is Getting Started – Mark Twain." *Quote Investigator*. 3 February 2018. https://bit.ly/36xL0zH.

Jobs, Steve. "Stanford University Commencement Address." 12 June 2005.

https://www.youtube.com/watch?v=UF8uR6Z6KLc.

CHAPTER 10   THE ROWING MARINE

"Lee Spencer: Amputee Marine from Devon breaks Atlantic row record." *BBC News*. 11 March 2019. https://bbc.in/2t5hy6w.

CHAPTER 11   THE HEROIC RWANDAN

"Homepage." Ikirezi Natural Products. 2019. https://www.ikirezi.com.

Allison, Scott; and Goethals, George. "How Hero Stories Energize Us." *Richmond*. 28 January 2015. https://bit.ly/2GxFKkR.

Bettelheim, Bruno. *The Uses of Enchantment: The Meaning and Importance of Fairy Tales*. New York: Vintage, 2010.

Allison, Scott; and Goethals, George. "Joseph Campbell: The Man Who Wrote the Book on Heroes." *Richmond*. 13 June 2012. https://bit.ly/37rxzTb.

Mcleod, Saul. "Erik Erirkson's Stages of Psychosocial Development." *Simply Psychology*. 2018. https://bit.ly/38HCwHD.

Haidt, Jonathan. "Elevation and the positive psychology of morality." *American Psychological Association*. 10 May 2001. https://bit.ly/3aQ8nYO.

CHAPTER 12   FRIENDS AND PARACHUTES

Kennedy, John F. "Landing a man on the Moon." Address to Congress. 25 May 1961. https://bit.ly/2Rw7HjC.

Wilford, John Nobel. "A Year later: Apollo's Message." *The New York Times*. 19 July 1970. https://nyti.ms/2O3VSyN.

Rath, Tom. *Vital Friends: The People You Can't Afford to Live Without*. Washington, DC: Gallup Press, 2006.

Anderson, Kare. "Who Packs Your Parachute?" *Forbes*. 18 November 2015. https://bit.ly/30XB4yc.

CHAPTER 13   FORMULAS AND TRICKS

"What Tiger said in his Masters winner's press conference." *Golf Channel Digital*. 14 April 2019. https://bit.ly/38Mpj0r.

Matthews, Gail. "Study Confirms Smart Strategies for Achieving Goals." *ScienceBeta*. 20 June 2013. https://sciencebeta.com/study-confirms-smart-strategies-for-achieving-goals/.

Ryback, Ralph. "The Science of Accomplishing Your Goals." *Psychology Today*. 3 October 2016. https://bit.ly/2Goovmf.

CHAPTER 14   RANDOM EVENTS

Ward, Marguerite. "Mark Zuckerberg Returns to the Harvard Dorm Room Where Facebook Was Born." *CNBC*. 25 May 2017. https://cnb.cx/2LLiT8n.

Hughes, Chris. *Fair Shot: Rethinking Inequality and How We Earn*. London: Bloomsbury, 2018.

Buffett, Warren. "Becoming Warren Buffett: Best 17 Quotes From the Oracle of Omaha." *Edgy Universe*. May 2017. https://bit.ly/2RZzvMm.

Payne, Roman. *Rooftop Soliloquy*. ModeRoom Press, 6 October 2009.

Kurt, Daniel. "Are You in the World's Top 1 Percent?" *Investopedia*. 15 September 2019. https://bit.ly/2QfDTYd.

Roser, Max; and Ortiz-Ospina, Esteban. "Tertiary Education." *Our World in Data*. 2019. https://bit.ly/2uF4jtO.

Bleiker, Carla. "UNESCO: 264 million children don't go to school." *Global Education Monitoring Report*. 24 October 2017. https://bit.ly/2U1LdZe.

Kyriacou, Nicole. "Project Literacy: Rewriting lives." Pearson, 22 March 2018. https://bit.ly/2XcK0OO.

Steindl-Rast, David. "Want to be happy? Be grateful." *TED Talk*. 27 November 2013. https://bit.ly/1m5MRCo.

CHAPTER 15   LEAVING THINGS BEHIND

Lang, Eugene. "Our History." *I Have a Dream Foundation*. 1981. https://bit.ly/2O3Z11x.

Green, Lyndsay. *The Well-Lived Life: Live With Purpose and Be Remembered*. New York: HarperCollins, 2019.

LAST PAGE

Tolkien, JRR. *The Fellowship of the Ring*. New York: HarperCollins, 2011 Edition.

ABOUT
THE AUTHOR

Neil Francis is the author of *Positive Thinking*, *The Entrepreneur's Book* and *Changing Course*. He is currently the chairman of a digital agency Pogo Studio, director of a software company, trustee of Chest, Heart and Stroke Scotland and a trustee of Sporting Memories. At the age of 41, he suffered a stroke that led him to discover a new, meaningful and rewarding life, which led Neil to publish four books and work with inspiring CEOs, leaders, charity bosses and entrepreneurs.

www.neil-francis.com
neil@neil-francis.com

ABOUT
THE BOOK

Inspired Thinking is an innovative way of discovering new ideas to achieve meaningful success. When someone or something inspires you, it pushes and propels you to do something new or different. It gives you new ideas and a strong feeling of enthusiasm and excitement. And this is the key point of this book; helping you discover inspiration from new ideas to positively change your life.

Each chapter is packed with new ideas from various sources of inspiration such as stories, practical examples, tips, tools and strategies, which will help you discover meaningful success. The book will explore ideas around personal value, individuality, risk, self-belief, triviality, purpose, staying young, proactivity, determination, heroes, goals, collaboration and legacy. *Inspired Thinking* is an important book for the 21st century, helping you to set the right goals and objectives to lead you on a journey of discovery, meaning, enjoyment and purpose.

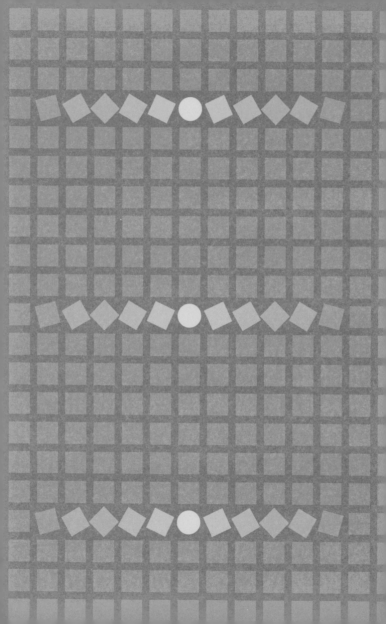

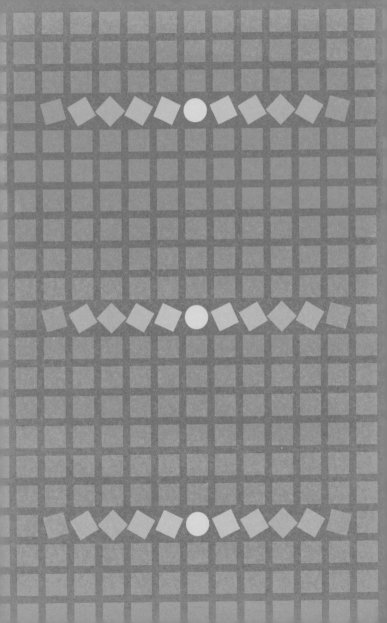